Old Indian Days

Part One
The Warrior

by

Charles A. Eastman

ABOUT THE AUTHOR

Charles Alexander Eastman (1858-1939), also known as Hakadah and later as Ohiyesa, was a prominent Native American author, physician, and activist. He was born in a Dakota Sioux community near Redwood Falls, Minnesota, to a mixed-race family of Dakota and European descent. Orphaned at an early age during the Dakota War of 1862, Eastman was raised in the traditional Dakota Sioux manner until the age of 15, when he attended formal schooling in the East. Eastman went on to become one of the first Native Americans to graduate from medical school, earning his medical degree from Boston University in 1889. He dedicated much of his life to advocating for Native American rights and education, working as a physician on reservations and serving as a government Indian inspector. Eastman is best known for his writings that aimed to preserve and promote understanding of Native American culture and history. His works include several books such as "Indian Boyhood" (1902), "Old Indian Days" (1907), and "The Soul of the Indian" (1911), which were instrumental in shaping non-Native perceptions of Native American life and spirituality. These books often drew from his personal experiences and upbringing, offering insights into traditional Dakota Sioux customs, spirituality, and values.

Charles A. Eastman's legacy extends beyond his literary contributions; he played a significant role in bridging cultural divides and promoting dialogue between Native and non-Native communities. His writings continue to be studied for their historical significance and their role in preserving Native American heritage.

CONTENTS

I
THE LOVE OF ANTELOPE

I

Upon a hanging precipice atop of the Eagle Scout Butte there appeared a motionless and solitary figure—almost eagle-like he perched! The people in the camp below saw him, but none looked at him long. They turned their heads quickly away with a nervous tingling, for the height above the plains was great. Almost spirit-like among the upper clouds the young warrior sat immovable.

It was Antelope. He was fasting and seeking a sign from the "Great Mystery," for such was the first step of the young and ambitious Sioux [who wished to be a noted warrior among his people].

He is a princely youth, among the wild Sioux, who hunts for his tribe and not for himself! His voice is soft and low at the campfire of his nation, but terror-giving in the field of battle. Such was Antelope's reputation. The more he sought the "Great Mystery" in solitude, the more gentle and retiring he became, and in the same proportion his courage and manliness grew. None could say that he was not a kind son and a good hunter, for he had already passed the "two-arrow-to-kill," his buffalo examination.

On a hot midsummer morning a few weeks later, while most of the inmates of the teepees were breakfasting in the open air, the powerful voice of the herald resounded among the pine-clad heights and green valleys.

"Hear ye, hear ye, warriors!" he chanted loudly. "The council has decreed that four brave young men must scout the country to the sunsetward of the camp, for the peace and protection of our people!"

All listened eagerly for the names of the chosen warriors, and in another moment there came the sonorous call: "Antelope, Antelope! the council has selected you!"

The camp was large—fully four hundred paces across; but in that country, in the clear morning air, such an announcement can be heard a great way, and in the silence that followed the hills repeated over and over the musical name of Antelope.

In due time the four chosen youths appeared before the council fire. The oath of the pipe was administered, and each took a few whiffs as reverently as a Churchman would partake of the sacrament. The chief of the council, who was old and of a striking appearance, gave the charge and command to the youthful braves.

There was a score or more of warriors ready mounted to escort them beyond the precincts of the camp, and the "fearless heart" song was sung according to the custom, as the four ran lightly from the door of the council teepee and disappeared in the woods.

It was a peculiarly trying and hazardous moment in which to perform the duties of a scout. The Sioux were encroaching upon the territory of hostile tribes, here in the foot-hills of the Big Horn Mountains, and now and then one of their hunters was cut off by the enemy. If continual vigilance could not save them, it might soon become necessary to retreat to their own hunting-grounds.

It was a savage fetish that a warrior must be proof against the alluring ways of pretty maidens; that he must place his honor far above the temptations of self-indulgence and indolence. Cold, hunger, and personal hardship did not count with Antelope when there was required of him any special exertion for the common good. It was cause to him of secret satisfaction that the council-men had selected him for a dangerous service in preference to some of his rivals and comrades.

He had been running for two or three hours at a good, even gait, and had crossed more than one of the smaller creeks, yet many deep gulches and bad lands lay between him and the furthest peak that melted into the blue dome above.

"I shall stand upon the Bear's Heart," he said to himself. "If I can do that, and still report before the others, I shall do well!" His keen eyes were constantly sweeping the country in his front, and suddenly he paused and shrank back motionless in a crouching attitude, still steadily keeping an eye upon a moving object. It was soon evident that some one was stealthily eying him from behind cover, and he was outwitted by the enemy! Still stooping, he glided down a little ravine, and as he reached the bed of the creek there emerged from it a large gray wolf.

This was very opportune for Antelope. He gave the gray wolf's danger-call with all his might; waited an instant and gave it a second time; then he turned and ran fleetly down the stream. At the same moment the wolf appeared upon the top of the bank, in full view of the enemy.

"Here he comes!" they whispered, and had their arrows on the string as the wolf trotted leisurely along, exposing only his head, for this was a common disguise among the plains Indians. But when he came out into the open, behold! it was only a gray wolf!

"Ugh!" the Utes grunted, as they looked at each other in much chagrin.

"Surely he was a man, and coming directly into our trap! We sang and prayed to the gods of war when our war chief sent us ahead to scout the Sioux people, to find their camp. This is a mystery, a magic! Either he is a Sioux in disguise, or we don't know their tricks!" exclaimed the leader.

Now they gave the war-whoop, and their arrows flew through the air. The wolf gave a yelp of distress, staggered and fell dead. Instantly they ran to examine the body, and found it to be truly that of a wolf.

"Either this is a wonderful medicine-man, or we are shamefully fooled by a Sioux warrior," they muttered.

They lost several minutes before they caught sight of Antelope, who had followed the bed of the creek as far as it lay in his direction and then came out of it at full speed. It would be safer for him to remain in concealment until dark; but in the meantime the Ute warriors would reach the camp, and his people were unprepared! It was necessary to expose himself to the enemy. He knew that it would be chiefly a contest of speed and he had an excellent start; but on the other hand, the Utes doubtless had their horses.

"The Sioux who played this trick on us must die to-day!" exclaimed their leader. "Come, friends, we cannot afford to let him tell this joke on us at the camp-fires of his people!"

Antelope was headed directly for Eagle Scout Butte, for the camp was in plain view from the top of this hill. He had run pretty much all day, but then, that was nothing!

"I shall reach the summit first, unless the Ute horses have wings!" he said to himself.

Looking over his shoulder, he saw five horsemen approaching, so he examined his bow and arrows as he ran.

"All is well," he muttered. "One of their spirits at the least must guide mine to the spirit land!" where, it was believed by them, there was no fighting.

Now he was within hearing of their whoops, but he was already at the foot of the butte. Their horses could not run up the steep ascent, and they were obliged to dismount. Like a deer the Sioux leaped from rock to rock, and almost within arrow-shot came his pursuers, wildly whooping and yelling.

When he had achieved the summit, he took his stand between two great rocks, and flashed his tiny looking-glass for a distress signal into the distant camp of his people.

For a long time no reply came, and many arrows flew over his head, as the Utes approached gradually from rock to rock. He, too, sent down a swift arrow now and then, to show them that he was no child or woman in fight, but brave as a bear when it is brought to bay.

"Ho, ho!" he shouted to the enemy, in token of a brave man's welcome to danger and death.

They replied with yells of triumph, as they pressed more and more closely upon him. One of their number had been dispatched to notify the main war-party when they first saw Antelope, but he did not know this, and his courage was undiminished. From time to time he continued to flash his signal, and at last like lightning the little white flash came in reply.

The sun was low when the besieged warrior discovered a large body of horsemen approaching from the northwest. It was the Ute warparty! He looked earnestly once more toward the Sioux camp, shading his eyes with his right palm. There, too, were many moving specks upon the plain, drawing toward the foot of the hill!

At the middle of the afternoon they had caught his distress signal, and the entire camp was thrown into confusion, for but few of the men had returned from the daily hunt. As fast as they came in, the warriors hurried away upon their best horses, singing and yelling. When they reached the well-known butte, towering abruptly in the midst of the plain, they could distinguish their enemies massed behind the hanging rocks and scattered cedar-trees, crawling up closer and closer, for the large warparty reached the hill just as the scouts who held Antelope at bay discovered the approach of his kinsmen.

Antelope had long since exhausted his quiver of arrows and was gathering up many of those that fell about him to send them back among his pursuers. When their attention was withdrawn from him for an instant by the sudden onset of the Sioux, he sprang to his feet.

He raised both his hands heavenward in token of gratitude for his rescue, and his friends announced with loud shouts the daring of Antelope.

Both sides fought bravely, but the Utes at last retreated and were fiercely pursued. Antelope stood at his full height upon the huge rock that had sheltered him, and gave his yell of defiance and exultation. Below him the warriors took it up, and among the gathering shadows the rocks echoed praises of his name.

In the Sioux camp upon Lost Water there were dances and praise songs, but there was wailing and mourning, too, for many lay dead among the crags. The name of Antelope was indelibly recorded upon Eagle Scout Butte.

"If he wished for a war-bonnet of eagle feathers, it is his to wear," declared one of the young men. "But he is modest, and scarcely even joins in the scalp dances. It is said of him that he has never yet spoken to any young woman!"

"True, it is not announced publicly that he has addressed a maiden. Many parents would like to have their daughters the first one he would speak to, but I am told he desires to go upon one or two more war-paths before seeking woman's company," replied another.

"Hun, hun, hay!" exclaimed a third youth ill-naturedly. He is already old enough to be a father!"

"This is told of him," rejoined the first speaker. "He wants to hold the record of being the young man who made the greatest number of coups before he spoke to a maiden. I know that there are not only mothers who would be glad to have him for a son-in-law, but their young daughters would not refuse to look upon the brave Antelope as a husband!"

It was true that in the dance his name was often mentioned, and at every repetition it seemed that the young women danced with more spirit, while even grandmothers joined in the whirl with a show of youthful abandon.

Wezee, the father of Antelope, was receiving congratulations throughout the afternoon. Many of the old men came to his lodge to smoke with him, and the host was more than gratified, for he was of a common family and had never before known what it is to bask in the sunshine of popularity and distinction. He spoke complacently as he crowded a handful of tobacco into the bowl of the long red pipe.

"Friends, our life here is short, and the life of a brave youth is apt to be shorter than most! We crave all the happiness that we can get, and it is right that we should do so. One who says that he does not care for reputation or success, is not likely to be telling the truth. So you will forgive me if I say too much about the honorable career of my son." This was the old man's philosophic apology.

"Ho, ho," his guests graciously responded. "It is your moon! Every moon has its fullness, when it lights up the night, while the little stars dance before it. So to every man there comes his full moon!"

Somewhat later in the day all the young people of the great camp were seen to be moving in one direction. All wore their best attire and finest ornaments, and even the parti-colored steeds were decorated to the satisfaction of their beauty-loving riders.

"Ugh, Taluta is making a maidens' feast! She, the prettiest of all the Unkpapa maidens!" exclaimed one of the young braves.

"She, the handsomest of all our young women!" repeated another.

Taluta was indeed a handsome maid in the height and bloom of womanhood, with all that wonderful freshness and magnetism which was developed and preserved by the life of the wilderness. She had already given five maidens' feasts, beginning with her fifteenth year, and her shy and diffident purity was held sacred by her people.

The maidens' circle was now complete. Behind it the outer circle of old women was equally picturesque and even more dignified. The grandmother, not the mother, was regarded as the natural protector of the young maiden, and the dowagers derived much honor from their position, especially upon public occasions, taking to themselves no small amount of credit for the good reputations of their charges.

Weshawee, whose protege had many suitors and was a decided coquette, fidgeted nervously and frequently adjusted her robe or fingered her necklace to ease her mind, for she dreaded lest, in spite of watchfulness, some mishap might have befallen her charge. Her anxiety was apparently shared by several other chaperons who stole occasional suspicious glances in the direction of certain of the young braves. It had been known to happen that a girl unworthy to join in the sacred feast was publicly disgraced.

A special police force was appointed to keep order on this occasion, each member of which was gorgeously painted and bedecked with eagle feathers, and carried in his hand a long switch with which to threaten the encroaching throng. Their horses wore head-skins of fierce animals to add to their awe-inspiring appearance.

The wild youths formed the outer circle of the gathering, attired like the woods in autumn, their long locks glossy with oil and perfumed with scented grass and leaves. Many pulled their blankets over their heads as if to avoid recognition, and loitered shyly at a distance.

Among these last were Antelope and his cousin, Red Eagle. They stood in the angle formed by the bodies of their steeds, whose noses were together. The young hero was completely enveloped in his handsome robe with a rainbow of bead-work acros the middle, and his small moccasined feet projected from beneath the lower border. Red Eagle held up an eagle-wing fan, partially concealing his face, and both gazed intently toward the center of the maidens' circle.

"Woo! woo!" was the sonorous exclamation of the police, announcing the beginning of the ceremonies. In the midst of the ring of girls stood the traditional heart-shaped red stone, with its bristling hedge of arrows. In this case there were five arrows, indicating that Taluta had already made as many maidens' feasts. Each of the maidens must lay her hand upon the stone in token of her purity and chastity, touching also as many arrows as she herself has attended maidens' feasts.

Taluta advanced first to the center. As she stood for a moment beside the sacred stone, she appeared to the gazing bystanders the embodiment of grace and modesty. Her gown, adorned with long fringes at the seams, was beaded in blue and white across the shoulders and half way to her waist. Her shining black hair was arranged in two thick plaits which hung down upon her bosom. There was a native dignity in her gestures and in her utterance of the maidens' oath, and as she turned to face the circle, all the other virgins followed her.

When the feast was ended and the gay concourse had dispersed, Antelope and his cousin were among the last to withdraw. The young man's eyes had followed every movement of Taluta as long as she remained in sight, and it was only when she vanished in the gathering shadows that he was willing to retire.

In savage courtship, it was the custom to introduce one's self boldly to the young lady, although sometimes it was convenient to have a sister introduce her brother. But Antelope had no sister to perform this office for him, and if he had had one, he would not have made the request. He did not choose to admit any one to his secret, for he had no confidence in himself or in the outcome of the affair. If it had been anything like trailing the doe, or scouting the Ojibway, he would have ridiculed the very notion of missing the object sought. But this was a new warfare—an unknown hunting! Although he was very anxious to meet Taluta, whenever the idea occurred to him he trembled like a leaf in the wind, and profuse perspiration rolled down his stoic visage. It was not customary to hold any social intercourse with the members of the opposite sex, and he had never spoken familiarly to any woman since he became a man, except his old grandmother. It was well known that the counsel of the aged brings luck to the youth in warfare and love.

Antelope arose early the next morning, and without speaking to any one he made a ceremonious toilet. He put on his finest buckskin shirt and a handsome robe, threw a beaded quiver over his shoulder, and walked directly away from the teepees and into the forest—he did not know why nor whither. The sounds of the camp grew fainter and fainter, until at last he found himself alone.

"How is it," mused the young man, "that I have hoped to become a leader among my people? My father is not a chief, and none of my ancestors were distinguished in war. I know well that, if I desire to be great, I must deny myself the pleasure of woman's company until I have made my reputation. I must not boast nor exhibit myself on my first success. The spirits do not visit the common haunts of men! All these rules I have thus far kept, and I must not now yield to temptation.... Man has much to weaken his ambition after he is married. A young man may seek opportunities to prove his worth, but to a married man the opportunity must come to try him. He acts only when compelled to act.... Ah, I must flee from the woman!... Besides, if she should like someone else better, I should be humiliated.... I must go upon a long war-path. I shall forget her...."

At this point his revery was interrupted by the joyous laughter of two young women. The melodious sing-song laughter of the Sioux maiden stirred the very soul of the young warrior.

All his philosophy deserted him, and he stood hesitating, looking about him as if for a chance of escape. A man who had never before felt the magnetic influence of woman in her simplicity and childlike purity, he became for the moment incapable of speech or action.

Meanwhile the two girls were wholly unconscious of any disturbing presence in the forest. They were telling each other the signals that each had received in the dance. Taluta's companion had stopped at the first raspberry bushes, while she herself passed on to the next thicket. When she emerged from the pines into an opening, she suddenly beheld Antelope, in his full-dress suit of courtship. Instantly she dropped her eyes.

Luckily the customs of courtship among the Sioux allow the covering of one's head with the blanket. In this attitude, the young man made a signal to Taluta with trembling fingers.

The wild red man's wooing was natural and straightforward; there was no circumspection, no maneuvering for time or advantage. Hot words of love burst forth from the young warrior's lips, with heavy breathing behind the folds of the robe with which he sought to shield his embarrassment.

"For once the spirits are guiding my fortunes! It may seem strange to you, when we meet thus by accident, that I should speak immediately of my love for you; but we live in a world where one must speak when the opportunity offers. I have thought much of you since I saw you at the maidens' feast.... Is Taluta willing to become the wife of Tatoka? The moccasins of her making will cause his feet to be swift in pursuit of the game, and on the trail of the enemy.... I beg of you, maiden, let our meeting be known only to the birds of the air, while you consider my proposal!"

All this while the maiden stood demurely at his side, playing with the lariat of her pony in her brown, fine hands. Her doeskin gown with profuse fringes hung gracefully as the drooping long leaves of the willow, and her two heavy braids of black hair, mingled with strings of deers' hoofs and wampum, fell upon her bosom. There was a faint glow underneath her brown skin, and her black eyes were calm and soft, yet full of native fire.

"You will not press for an answer now," she gently replied, without looking at him. "I expected to see no one here, and your words have taken me by surprise.... I grant your last request. The birds alone can indulge in gossip about our meeting,—unless my cousin, who is in the next ravine, should see us together!" She sprang lightly upon the back of her pony, and disappeared among the scattered pines.

Between the first lovers' meeting and the second was a period of one moon. This was wholly the fault of Antelope, who had been a prey to indecision and painful thoughts. Half regretting his impulsive declaration, and hoping to forget his pangs in the chances of travel and war, he had finally enlisted in the number of those who were to go with the war-leader Crowhead into the Ute country. As was the custom of the Sioux warriors upon the eve of departure, the young men consulted their spiritual advisers, and were frequently in the purifying vapor-bath, and fasting in prayer.

The last evening had come, and Antelope was on the way to the top of the hill behind the camp for a night of prayer. Suddenly in the half-light he came full upon Taluta, leading her pony down the narrow trail. She had never looked more beautiful to the youth than at that moment.

"Ho," he greeted her. She simply smiled shyly.

"It is long since we met," he ventured.

"I have concluded that you do not care to hear my reply," retorted the girl.

"I have nothing to say in my defense, but I hope that you will be generous. I have suffered much.... You will understand why I stand far from you," he added gently. "I have been preparing myself to go upon the warpath. We start at daylight for the Ute country. Every day for ten days I have been in the vapor-bath, and ten nights fasting."

As Taluta well knew, a young warrior under these circumstances dared not approach a woman, not even his own wife.

"I still urge you to be my wife. Are you ready to give me your answer?" continued Antelope.

"My answer was sent to you by your grandmother this very day," she replied softly.

"Ah, tell me, tell me,..." pressed the youth eagerly.

"All is well. Fear nothing," murmured the maiden.

"I have given my word—I have made my prayers and undergone purification. I must not withdraw from this war-path," he said after a silence. "But I know that I shall be fortunate!... My grandmother will give you my love token.... Ah, kechuwa (dear love)! watch the big star every night! I will watch it, too—then we shall both be watching! Although far apart, our spirits will be together."

The moon had risen above the hill, and the cold light discovered the two who stood sadly apart, their hearts hot with longing. Reluctantly, yet without a backward look or farewell gesture, the warrior went on up the hill, and the maiden hurried homeward. Only a few moments before she had been happy in the anticipation of making her lover happy. The truth was she had been building air-castles in the likeness of a white teepee pitched upon a virgin prairie all alone, surrounded by mountains. Tatoka's war-horse and hunting pony were picketed near by, and there she saw herself preparing the simple meal for him! But now he has clouded her dreams by this untimely departure.

"He is too brave.... His life will be a short one," she said to herself with foreboding.

For a few hours all was quiet, and just before the appearance of day the warriors' departure was made known by their farewell songs. Antelope was in the line early, but he was heavy of heart, for he knew that his sweetheart was sorely puzzled and disappointed by his abrupt departure. His only consolation was the knowledge that he had in his bundle a pair of moccasins made by her hands. He had not yet seen them, because it was the custom not to open any farewell gifts until the first camp was made, and then they must be opened before the eyes of all the young men! It brings luck to the war-party, they said. He would have preferred to keep his betrothal secret, but there was no escaping the custom.

All the camp-fires were burning and supper had been eaten, when the herald approached every group and announced the programme for the evening. It fell to Antelope to open his bundle first. Loud laughter pealed forth when the reluctant youth brought forth a superb pair of moccasins— the recognized lovegift! At such times the warriors' jokes were unmerciful, for it was considered a last indulgence in jesting, perhaps for many moons. The recipient was well known to be a novice in love, and this token first disclosed the fact that he had at last succumbed to the allurements of woman. When he sang his love-song he was obliged to name the giver of the token, and many a disappointed suitor was astonished to hear Taluta's name.

It was a long journey to the Ute country, and when they reached it there was a stubbornly contested fight. Both sides claimed the victory, and both lost several men. Here again Antelope was signally favored by the gods of war. He counted many coups or blows, and exhibited his bravery again and again in the charges, but he received no wound.

On the return journey Taluta's beautiful face was constantly before him. He was so impatient to see her that he hurried on in advance of his party, when they were still several days' travel from the Sioux camp.

"This time I shall join in all the dances and participate in the rejoicings, for she will surely like to have me do so," he thought to himself. "She will join also, and I know that none is a better dancer than Taluta!"

In fancy, Antelope was practicing the songs of victory as he rode alone over the vast wild country.

He had now passed Wild Horse Creek and the Black Hills lay to the southeast, while the Big Horn range loomed up to the north in gigantic proportions. He felt himself at home.

"I shall now be a man indeed. I shall have a wife!" he said aloud.

At last he reached the point from which he expected to view the distant camp. Alas, there was no camp there! Only a solitary teepee gleamed forth upon the green plain, which was almost surrounded by a quick turn of the River of Deep Woods. The teepee appeared very white. A peculiar tingling sensation passed through his frame, and the pony whinnied often as he was urged forward at a gallop.

When Antelope beheld the solitary teepee he knew instantly what it was. It was a grave! Sometimes a new white lodge was pitched thus for the dead, who lay in state within upon a couch of finest skins, and surrounded by his choicest possessions.

Antelope's excitement increased as he neared the teepee, which was protected by a barricade of thick brush. It stood alone and silent in the midst of the deserted camp. He kicked the sides of his tired horse to make him go faster. At last he jumped from the saddle and ran toward the door. There he paused for a moment, and at the thought of desecrating a grave, a cold terror came over him.

"I must see—I must see!" he said aloud, and desperately he broke through the thorny fence and drew aside the oval swinging door.

II

In the stately white teepee, seen from afar, both grave and monument, there lay the fair body of Taluta! The bier was undisturbed, and the maiden looked beautiful as if sleeping, dressed in her robes of ceremony and surrounded by all her belongings.

Her lover looked upon her still face and cried aloud. "Hey, hey, hey! Alas! alas! If I had known of this while in the Ute country, you would not be lonely on the spirit path."

He withdrew, and laid the doorflap reverently back in its place. How long he stood without the threshold he could not tell. He stood with head bowed down upon his breast, tearless and motionless, utterly oblivious to everything save the bier of his beloved. His charger grazed about for a long time where he had left him, but at last he endeavored by a low whinny to attract his master's attention, and Antelope awoke from his trance of sorrow.

The sun was now hovering over the western ridges. The mourner's throat was parched, and perspiration rolled down his cheeks, yet he was conscious of nothing but a strong desire to look upon her calm, sweet face once more.

He kindled a small fire a little way off, and burned some cedar berries and sweet-smelling grass. Then he fumigated himself thoroughly to dispel the human atmosphere, so that the spirit might not be offended by his approach, for he greatly desired to obtain a sign from her spirit. He had removed his garments and stood up perfectly nude save for the breechclout. His long hair was unbraided and hung upon his shoulders, veiling the upper half of his splendid body. Thus standing, the lover sang a dirge of his own making. The words were something like this:

Ah, spirit, thy flight is mysterious!

While the clouds are stirred by our wailing,

And our tears fall faster in sorrow —

While the cold sweat of night benumbs us,

Thou goest alone on thy journey,

In the midst of the shining star people!

Thou goest alone on thy journey —

Thy memory shall be our portion;

Until death we must watch for the spirit!

The eyes of Antelope were closed while he chanted the dirge. He sang it over and over, pausing between the lines, and straining as it were every sense lest he might not catch the rapt whisper of her spirit, but only the distant howls of coyotes answered him. His body became cold and numb from sheer exhaustion, and at last his knees bent under him and he sank down upon the ground, still facing the teepee. Unconsciousness overtook him, and in his sleep or trance the voice came:

"Do not mourn for me, my friend! Come into my teepee, and eat of my food."

It seemed to Antelope that he faltered for a moment; then he entered the teepee. There was a cheerful fire burning in the center. A basin of broiled buffalo meat was placed opposite the couch of Taluta, on the other side of the fire. Its odor was delicious to him, yet he hesitated to eat of it.

"Fear not, kechuwa (my darling)! It will give you strength," said the voice.

The maid was natural as in life. Beautifully attired, she sat up on her bed, and her demeanor was cheerful and kind.

The young man ate of the food in silence and without looking at the spirit. "Ho, kechuwa!" he said to her when returning the dish, according to the custom of his people.

Silently the two sat for some minutes, while the youth gazed into the burning embers.

"Be of good heart," said Taluta, at last, "for you shall meet my twin spirit! She will love you as I do, and you will love her as you love me. This was our covenant before we came into this world."

The conception of a "twin spirit" was familiar to the Sioux. "Ho," responded the warrior, with dignity and all seriousness. He felt a great awe for the spirit, and dared not lift his eyes to her face.

"Weep no more, kechuwa, weep no more," she softly added; and the next moment Antelope found himself outside the mysterious teepee. His limbs were stiff and cold, but he did not feel faint nor hungry. Having filled his pipe, he held it up to the spirits and then partook of the smoke; and thus revived, he slowly and reluctantly left the sacred spot.

The main war-party also visited the old camp and saw the solitary teepee grave, but did not linger there. They continued on the trail of the caravan until they reached the new camping ground. They called themselves successful, although they had left several of their number on the field. Their triumph songs indicated this; therefore the people hurried to receive the news and to learn who were the unfortunates.

The father of Antelope was foremost among those who ran to meet the war-party. He learned that his son had distinguished himself in the fight, and that his name was not mentioned among the brave dead.

"And where, then, is he?" he asked, with unconcealed anxiety.

"He left us three days ago to come in advance," they replied.

"But he has not arrived!" exclaimed old Wezee, in much agitation.

He returned to his teepee, where he consoled himself as best he could by smoking the pipe in solitude. He could neither sing praises nor indulge in the death dirge, and none came in either to congratulate or mourn with him.

The sun had disappeared behind the hills, and the old man still sat gazing into the burning embers, when he heard a horse's footfall at the door of his lodge.

"Ho, atay (father)!" came the welcome call.

"Mechinkshe! mechinkshe!" (my son, my son), he replied in unrestrained joy. Old Wezee now stood on the threshold and sang the praise song for his son, ending with a warwhoop such as he had not indulged in since he was quite a young man.

The camp was once more alive with the dances, and the dull thud of the Indian drum was continually in the air. The council had agreed that Antelope was entitled to wear a war-bonnet of eagles' feathers. He was accordingly summoned before the aboriginal parliament, and from the wise men of the tribe he received his degree of war-bonnet.

It was a public ceremony. The great pipe was held up for him to take the smoke of high honor.

The happiest person present was the father of Antelope; but he himself remained calm and unmoved throughout the ceremony.

"He is a strange person," was the whisper among a group of youths who were watching the proceedings with envious eyes.

The young man was strangely listless and depressed in spirit. His old grandmother knew why, but none of the others understood. He never joined in the village festivities, while the rest of his family were untiring in the dances, and old Wezee was at the height of his happiness.

It was a crisp October morning, and the family were eating their breakfast of broiled bison meat, when the large drum at the council lodge was struck three times. The old man set down his wooden basin.

"Ah, my son, the war-chiefs will make an announcement! It may be a call for the enlistment of warriors! I am sorry," he said, and paused. "I am sorry, because I would rather no war-party went out at present. I am getting old. I have enjoyed your success, my son. I love to hear the people speak your name. If you go again upon the war-path, I shall no longer be able to join in the celebrations. Something tells me that you will not return!"

Young braves were already on their way to the council lodge. Tatoka looked, and the temptation was great.

"Father, it is not becoming for me to remain at home when others go," he said, at last.

"Ho," was the assent uttered by the father, with a deep sigh.

"Five hundred braves have enlisted to go with the great war prophet against the three confederated tribes," he afterward reported at home, with an air of elation which he had not worn for some moons.

Since Antelope had received the degree of war-bonnet, his father had spared neither time nor his meager means in his behalf. He had bartered his most cherished possessions for several eagles that were brought in by various hunters of the camp, and with his own hands had made a handsome war-bonnet for his son.

"You will now wear a war-bonnet for the first time, and you are the first of our family who has earned the right to wear one for many generations. I am proud of you, my son," he said as he presented it.

But when the youth replied: "Ho, ho, father! I ought to be a brave man in recognition of this honor," he again sighed heavily.

"It is that I feared, my son! Many a young man has lost his life for vanity and love of display!"

The evening serenades began early, for the party was to leave at once. In groups upon their favorite ponies the warriors rode around the inner circle of the great camp, singing their war-songs. All the people came out of the teepees, and sitting by twos and threes upon the ground, bedecked with savage finery, they watched and listened. The pretty wild maidens had this last opportunity given them to look upon the faces of their sweethearts, whom they might never see again. Here and there an old man was singing the gratitude song or thank-offering, while announcing the first warpath of a novice, for such an announcement meant the giving of many presents to the poor and aged. So the camp was filled with songs of joy and pride in the departing husbands, brothers, and sons.

As soon as darkness set in the sound of the rude native flute was added to the celebration. This is the lover's farewell. The young braves, wrapped from head to foot in their finest robes, each sounded the plaintive strains near the teepee of the beloved. The playful yodeling of many voices in chorus was heard at the close of each song.

At midnight the army of five hundred, the flower of the Sioux, marched against their ancient enemy. Antelope was in the best of spirits. He had his war-bonnet to display before the enemy! He was now regarded as one of the foremost warriors of his band, and might probably be asked to perform some specially hazardous duty, so that he was fully prepared to earn further distinction.

In five days the Sioux were encamped within a day's travel of the permanent village of the confederated tribes—the Rees, Mandans, and Gros Ventres. The war-chief selected two men, Antelope and Eaglechild, to scout at night in advance of the main force. It was thought that most of the hunters had already returned to their winter quarters, and in this case the Sioux would have no mean enemy to face. On the other hand, a battle was promised that would enlarge their important traditions.

The two made their way as rapidly as possible toward the ancestral home of their enemies. It was a night perfectly suited to what they had to do, for the moon was full, the fleeting clouds hiding it from time to time and casting deceptive shadows.

When they had come within a short distance of the lodges unperceived, they lay flat for a long time, and studied the ways of the young men in every particular, for it was Antelope's plan to enter the great village and mingle boldly with its inhabitants. Even their hoots and love-calls were carefully noted, so that they might be able to imitate them. There were several entertainments in progress in different parts of the village, yet it was apparent that the greatest vigilance was observed. The lodges of poles covered with earth were partly underground, and at one end the war-horses were stabled, as a precaution against a possible surprise.

At the moment that a large cloud floated over the moon, casting a shadow large enough to cover the entire village, the drum in one of the principal lodges was struck in quick time, accompanied by boisterous war-whoops and singing. The two scouts adjusted their robes about them in the fashion of the strangers, and walked openly in that direction.

They glanced quickly from side to side as they approached, but no one paid any attention, so they came up with other young men and peeped through the chinks in the earth wigwam. It was a great gambling party. Among the guests were several distinguished warriors, and each at an opportune time would rise and recount his great deeds in warfare against the Sioux. The strangers could read their gestures, and Antelope was once or twice almost on the point of stringing his bow to send an arrow through the audacious speaker.

As they moved about the village, taking note of its numbers and situation, and waiting an opportunity to withdraw without exciting suspicion, they observed some of the younger braves standing near another large wigwam, and one or two even peeped within. Moved by sudden curiosity, Antelope followed their example. He uttered a low exclamation and at once withdrew.

"What is it?" asked his companion, but received no answer.

It was evidently the home of a chief. The family were seated within at their usual occupations, and the bright light of the central fire shone full upon the face of a most lovely maiden.

Antelope stood apparently motionless, but he was trembling under his robe like a leaf.

"Come, friend, there is another large cloud almost over the moon! We must move away under its concealing shadow," urged Eaglechild.

The other stood still as if undecided, but at last he approached the lodge and looked in a second time. There sat his sweetheart in human form once more! The maiden was attired in a doeskin gown set with elk's teeth like ivory. Her eyes were cast down demurely over her embroidery, but in every feature she was the living counterpart of Taluta!

At last the two got away unobserved, and hastened toward the place where they had concealed their horses. But here Antelope sent his companion on in advance, making the excuse that he wished to study further the best position from which to make the attack.

When he was left alone he stood still for a moment to decide upon a plan. He could think of nothing but that he must meet the Ree maiden before daylight! He realized the extreme hazard of the attempt, but he also recalled what he had been told by the spirit of Taluta, and the supernatural command seemed to justify him even in going thus upon the eve of battle to meet the enemy of his people.

He skirted the heavy timber and retraced his steps to a point from which he could see the village. The drum of the gambling party had ceased with the shouts and laughter of the players. Apparently the village was lost in slumber. The moon had set, and without pausing he advanced to the home of the girl. As he came near some dogs began to bark, but he silenced them after the manner of the Rees, and they obeyed him.

When Antelope softly raised the robe that hung over the entrance to the chief's lodge, he saw the fire smoldering in the center, and the members of the household lying in their respective places, all seemingly in a deep sleep. The girl lay opposite the entrance, where he had seen her seated in the early part of the evening.

The heart of the Sioux beat violently, and he glanced nervously to left and right. There was neither sound nor movement. Then he pulled his robe completely over his head, after the fashion of a Ree lover, and softly entered the wigwam.

The Ree maiden, having industriously worked on her embroidery until far into the night, had retired to rest. In her dreams, the twin sister came to her of whom she had had visions ever since she could remember, and especially when something of importance was about to happen.

This time she came with a handsome young man of another tribe, and said: "Sister, I bring you a Sioux, who will be your husband!"

The dreamer opened her eyes to behold a youth bending over her and gently pulling her robe, as a suitor is permitted to do to awaken his beloved.

When he saw that she was awake, the Sioux touched his breast, saying in a whisper, "Tatoka," and made the sign for Antelope. This pleased the Ree girl, for her own brother, who had died the year before, had borne that name. She immediately sat up and stirred the embers into a light blaze. Then she took hold of his blanket and drew it from his face; and there she seemed to see the very features of the man of her vision!

He took her hand in his, and she felt the force of love stream through his long, nervous fingers, and instinctively knew his thoughts. In her turn she touched her breast and made the sign for Shield, pronouncing in her own tongue the word, Stasu. This seemed to him also a name of good omen, and in the sign language which was common to all the people of the plains, he asked her to be his wife.

Vividly her dream came back to her, and she could not refuse the stranger. Her soul already responded to his; and for a few minutes they sat silently side by side. When he arose and beckoned, "Come with me," she had no question to make, and without a word she followed him from her father's lodge and out into the forest.

In the midst of his ascending fame, at a moment when opportunity seemed to favor his ambition, the brave Antelope had mysteriously disappeared! His companion scout returned with a favorable report. He said that the men of the three confederated tribes were gambling and feasting, wholly unconscious of danger, and that Antelope would follow him with a further report upon the best point of attack. The red warriors impatiently awaited his return, until it became apparent that they could wait no longer without sacrificing their chance of success. When the attack was made it was already rather late. The sun had fairly cleared the eastern hills, and most of the men were outside their lodges.

It was a great battle! Again and again the Sioux were repulsed, but as often they rallied and repeated the charge until sundown, when they effected their retreat with considerable loss. Had Antelope returned in due season, the charge would have been made before dawn, while the people were yet asleep.

When the battle was over, the Rees, Mandans, and Gros Ventres gathered their dead and wounded. The night was filled with mourning. Soon the sad news was heralded throughout the camp that the beautiful daughter of the Ree chief was among the missing. It was supposed that she must have been captured while driving her ponies to water in the early morning. The grief for her loss was mingled with horror, because of a fear that she might suffer humiliation at the hands of the Sioux warriors, and among the young men there were muttered threats that the Sioux would pay dearly for this.

Though partially successful, the Sioux had lost many of their bravest warriors, and none could tell what had happened to Antelope—he who had been believed the favorite of the gods of war. It was suggested by some envious ones that perhaps he had recognized the strongly entrenched position of the three tribes, and believing the battle would be a disastrous one, had set out for home without making his report. But this supposition was not deemed credible. On the other hand, the idea was entertained that he had reentered the village, was detected and slain; and therefore the enemy was on the lookout when the attack was made.

"Hay, hay, hay, mechinkshe (Alas, alas, my son)!" was the sorrowful cry with which his old father received the news. His head fell upon his breast, and all the others groaned in sympathy.

The sunset sky was a blanket of beautiful painting. There were camp-fires among the clouds in orange and scarlet, while some were black as night. So the camp fairly glowed in celebration of its heroes; yet there was deep grief in many families. When the evening meal had been eaten and the people were sitting outside their lodges, a tall old man, almost nude, appeared in the circle, riding a fine horse. He had blackened his face, his hair was cut short, and the horse also had been deprived of his flowing mane and tail. Both were in deep mourning, after the fashion of the Sioux.

"Ho ho!" exclaimed many warriors as he passed them, singing in a hoarse, guttural voice.

"Ugh, he sings a war-song!" remarked one.

"Yes, I am told that he will find his son's bones, or leave his own in the country of the enemy!"

The rain had fallen incessantly for two days. The fleeing lovers had reached this lonely mountain valley of the Big Horn region on the night that the cold fall rains set in, and Antelope had hurriedly constructed an arbor house or rude shelter of pine and cedar boughs.

It was enough. There they sat, man and wife, in their first home of living green! The cheerful fire was burning in the center, and the happy smoke went straight up among the tall pines. There was no human eye to gaze upon them to embarrass—not even a common language in which to express their love for one another.

Their marriage, they believed, was made by a spirit, and it was holy in their minds. Each had cast away his people and his all for the sake of this emotion which had suddenly overtaken them both with overwhelming force, and the warrior's ambition had disappeared before it like a morning mist before the sun.

To them a new life was just beginning, and they had all but forgotten the existence of any world save this. The young bride was enshrined in a bower of spicy fragrance, and her face shone whenever her eyes met those of her husband.

"This is as I would have it, kechuwa (darling)!" exclaimed the Sioux in his own language. She simply responded with a childlike smile. Although she did not understand his words, she read in the tones of his voice only happy and loving thoughts.

The Ree girl had prepared a broiled bison steak, and her husband was keeping the fire well fed with dry fagots. The odor of the buming fat was delicious, and the gentle patter of the rain made a weird music outside their wigwam.

As soon as her husband had left her alone—for he must go to water the ponies and conceal them at a distance—Stasu came out to collect more wood. Instinctively she looked all about her. Huge mountains towered skyward, clad in pines. The narrow valley in which she was wound its way between them, and on every side there was heavy forest.

She stood silent and awed, scarcely able to realize that she had begun her new life absolutely alone, with no other woman to advise or congratulate her, and visited only by the birds of the air. Yet all the world to her just now was Antelope! No other woman could smile on him. He could not talk to any one but her. The evening drum at the council lodge could not summon him away from her, and she was well content.

When the young wife had done everything she could think of in preparation for her husband's return, including the making of several birch-bark basins and pails for water, the rain had quite ceased, so she spread her robe just outside the lodge and took up her work-bag, in which she had several pairs of moccasin-tops already beaded.

While she bent over her work, getting up from time to time to turn the roast which she had impaled upon a sharp stick above the glowing coals, the bride had a stream of shy callers, of the little people of the woods. She sat very still, so as not to startle them, and there is much curiosity among these people concerning a stranger.

Presently she was startled by a footfall not unlike that of a man. She had not been married long enough to know the sound of her husband's step, and she felt a thrill of joy and fear alternately. It might be he, and it might be a stranger! She was loath to look up, but at last gave a furtive glance, and met squarely the eyes of a large grizzly bear, who was seated upon his haunches not far away.

Stasu was surprised, but she showed no fear; and fearlessness is the best shield against wild animals. In a moment she got up unconcernedly, and threw a large piece of meat to the stranger.

"Take of my wedding feast, O great Bear!" she addressed him, "and be good to me to bless my first teepee! O be kind and recognize my brave act in taking for my husband one of the warriors of the Sioux, the ancient enemy of my people! I have accepted a husband of a language other than mine, and am come to live among you as your neighbor. I offer you my friendship!"

The bear's only answer to her prayer was a low growl, but having eaten the meat, he turned and clumsily departed.

In the meantime Antelope had set himself to master the geography of that region, to study the outlook for game, and ascertain the best approaches to their secret home. It was already settled in his mind that he could never return either to his wife's people or to his own. His fellow-warriors would not forgive his desertion, and the Rees could not be expected to welcome as a kinsman one of the foremost of their ancient foes. There was nothing to be done but to remain in seclusion, and let them say what they would of him!

He had loved the Ree maiden from the first moment he beheld her by the light of the blazing embers, and that love must satisfy him. It was well that he had never cared much for company, but had spent many of his young days in solitude and fasting. It did not seem at all strange to him that he had been forced to retreat into an unknown and wild country with a woman whom he saw in the evening for the first time, and fled with as his own wife before sunrise!

By the afternoon he had thoroughly informed himself upon the nature of the surrounding country. Everything on the face of the map was surveyed and charted in his mind, in accordance with his habits and training. This done, he turned toward his secret dwelling. As he walked rapidly and noiselessly through the hidden valleys and along the singing streams, he noticed fresh signs of the deer, elk, and other wild tribes among whom he had chosen to abide. "They shall be my people," he said to himself.

Behind a group of cedars he paused to reconnoiter, and saw the pine-bough wigwam like a giant plant, each row of boughs overlapping the preceding circular row like the scales of a fish. Stasu was sitting before it upon a buffalorobe, attired in her best doeskin gown. Her delicate oval face was touched with red paint, and her slender brown hands were occupied with a moccasin meant for him to wear. He could scarcely believe that it was a mortal woman that he saw before him in broad day—the pride of No Man's Trail, for that is what the Crow Indians call that valley!

"Ho, ho, kechuwa!" he exclaimed as he approached her, and her heart leaped in recognition of the magnetic words of love.

"It is good that we are alone! I shall never want to go back to my people so long as I have you. I can dwell here with you forever, unless you should think otherwise!" she exclaimed in her own tongue, accompanied by graphic signs.

"Ho, I think of nothing else! I can see in every creature only friendly ways and good feeling. We can live alone here, happily, unless you should feel differently," he replied in his own language with the signs, so that his bride understood him.

The environment was just what it should be when two people are united in marriage. The wedding music was played by Nature, and trees, brooks, and the birds of the air contributed their peculiar strains to a great harmony. All of the people on No Man's Trail were polite, and understood the reserves of love. These two had yielded to a simple and natural impulse; but its only justification to their minds was the mysterious leading of the twin spirit! That was the sum total of their excuse, and it was enough.

Before the rigor of winter had set in, Tatoka brought to his bride many buffalo skins. She was thoroughly schooled in the arts of savage womanhood; in fact, every Indian maid was trained with this thought in view—that she should become a beautiful, strong, skillful wife and mother—the mother of a noble race of warriors!

In a short time within that green and pine-scented enclosure there smiled a little wild paradise. Hard by the pine-bough wigwam there stood a new white buffalo-skin teepee, tanned, cut, sewed, and pitched by the hands of Stasu. Away in the woods, down by the rushing brook, was her tannery, and not far away, in a sunny, open spot, she prepared her sun-cured meats for winter use. Her kitchen was a stone fireplace in a shady spot, and her parlor was the lodge of evergreen, overhung on two sides by inaccessible ledges, and bounded on the other two by the sparkling stream. It was a secret place, and yet a citadel; a silent place, and yet not lonely!

The winter was cold and long, but the pair were happy in one another's company, and accepted their strange lot as one that was chosen for them by the spirits. Stasu had insisted upon her husband speaking to her in his own language, that she might learn it quickly. In a little while she was able to converse with him, and when she had acquired his language she taught him hers.

While Antelope was occupied with hunting and exploring the country, always keeping in mind the danger of discovery by some wandering scout or hunter, his wife grew well acquainted with the wild inhabitants of No Man's Trail. These people are as full of curiosity as man, and as the Sioux never hunted near his home, they were entirely fearless. Many came to the door of Stasu's lodge, and she was not afraid, but offered them food and spoke to them kindly. All animals judge by signs and are quick in reading tones and gestures; so that the Ree girl soon had grandfathers and grandmothers, after the Indian fashion, among the wolves and bears that came oftenest for food.

Her husband in the field had also his fellow-hunters and friends. When he killed the buffalo he always left enough meat for the wolves, the eagles, and the ravens to feast upon, and these watched for the coming of the lonely wild man. More than once they told him by their actions of the presence of a distant campfire, but in each instance it proved to be a small war-party which had passed below them on the trail.

Again it was summer. Never had the mountains looked grander or more mysterious to the eyes of the two. The valley was full of the music and happiness of the winged summer people; the trees wore their summer attire, and the meadow its green blanket. There were many homes made happy by the coming of little people everywhere, but no pair was happier than Stasu and her husband when one morning they saw their little brave lying wrapped in soft deerskins, and heard for the first time his plaintive voice!

That morning, when Antelope set out on the hunt, he stopped at the stream and looked at himself seriously to see whether he had changed since the day before. He must now appear much graver, he said to himself, because he is the father of a new man!

In spite of himself, his thoughts were with his own people, and he wondered what his old grandmother would have said to his child! He looked away off toward the Black Hills, to the Sioux country, and in his heart he said, "I am a coward!"

The boy grew naturally, and never felt the lack of playmates and companions, for his mother was ingenious in devising plays for him, and in winning for him the confidence and kindness of the animal friends. He was the young chief and the hero of No Man's Trail! The bears and wolves were his warriors; the buffalo and elk the hostile tribes upon whom he went to war. Small as he was, he soon preferred to roam alone in the woods. His parents were often anxious, but, on the other hand, they entertained the hope that he would some day be "wakan," a mysterious or supernatural man, for he was getting power from his wild companions and from the silent forces of nature.

One day, when he was about five years old, he gave a dance for his wild pets upon the little plateau which was still their home. He had clothed Mato, the bear, in one of his father's suits as a great medicine-man. Waho, the wolf, was painted up as a brave; and the young buffalo calf was attired in one of his mother's gowns. The boy acted as chief and master of ceremonies.

The savage mother watched him with undisguised pride, mingled with sorrow. Tears coursed down her dusky cheeks, although at the same time she could not help laughing heartily at the strange performance. When the play was ended, and she had served the feast at its close, Stasu seemed lost in thought.

"He should not live in this way," she was saying to herself. "He should know the traditions and great deeds of my people! Surely his grandfather would be proud of the boy!"

That evening, while the boy slept, and Mato lay outside the lodge eagerly listening and sniffing the night air, the parents sat silent and ill at ease. After a long time Stasu spoke her mind.

"My husband, you ask me why I am sad. It is because I think that the Great Mystery will be displeased if we keep this little boy forever in the wilderness. It is wrong to allow him to grow up among wild animals; and if sickness or accident should deprive him of his father and mother, our spirits would never rest, because we had left him alone! I have decided to ask you to take us back, either to your people or to my people. We must sacrifice our pride, or, if needs be, our lives, for his life and happiness!"

This speech of Stasu's was a surprise to her husband. His eyes rested upon the ground as he listened, and his face assumed the proverbial stoical aspect, yet in it there was not lacking a certain nobleness. At last he lifted his eyes to hers, and said:

"You have spoken wise words, and it shall be as you have said. We shall return to your people. If I am to die at the hands of the ancient enemy of the Sioux, I shall die because of my love for you, and for our child. But I cannot go back to my own people to be ridiculed by unworthy young men for yielding to love of a Ree maiden!"

There was much feeling behind these words of Antelope. The rigid customs of his people are almost a religion, and there is one thing above all else which a Sioux cannot bear—that is the ridicule of his fellow-warriors. Yes, he can endure severe punishment or even death at the hands of the enemy rather than a single laugh of derision from a Sioux!

In a few days the household articles were packed, and the three sadly turned their backs upon their home. Stasu and her husband were very silent as they traveled slowly along. When they reached the hill called "Born-of-Day," and she saw from its summit the country of her people lying below her, she cried aloud, weeping happy tears. Antelope sat near by with bowed head, silently smoking.

Finally on the fifth day they arrived within sight of the great permanent village of the three tribes. They saw the earth lodges as of old, thickly clustered along the flats of the Missouri, among their rustling maize-fields. Antelope stopped. "I think you had better give me something to eat, woman," he said, smiling. It was the Sioux way of saying, "Let me have my last meal!"

After they had eaten, Stasu opened her buckskin bags and gave her husband his finest suit. He dressed himself carefully in the fashion of his tribe, putting on all the feathers to which he was entitled as a warrior. The boy also was decked out in gala attire, and Stasu, the matron, had never looked more beautiful in her gown of ceremony with the decoration of elks' teeth, the same that she had worn on the evening of her disappearance.

As she dressed herself, the unwelcome thought forced itself upon her,—"What if my love is killed by my own countrymen in their frenzy? This beautiful gown must then give place to a poor one, and this hair will be cut short!" for such is the mourning of the widow among her people.

The three rode openly down the long slope, and were instantly discovered by the people of the village. Soon the plain was black with the approaching riders. Stasu had begged her husband to remain behind, while she went on alone with the boy to obtain forgiveness, but he sternly refused, and continued in advance. When the foremost Ree warriors came within arrow-shot they began to shoot, to which he paid no attention.

But the child screamed with terror, and Stasu cried out in her own tongue:

"Do not shoot! I am the daughter of your chief!"

One of them returned the reply: "She is killed by the Sioux!" But when the leaders saw her plainly they were astounded.

For a time there was great confusion. Some held that they should all die, for the woman had been guilty of treason to her people, and even now she might be playing a trick upon them. Who could say that behind that hill there was not a Sioux war-party?

"No, no," replied others. "They are in our power. Let them tell their story!"

Stasu told it simply, and said in conclusion:

"This man, one of the bravest and most honorable men of his tribe, deserted on the night of the attack, and all because he loved a Ree maiden!

He now comes to be your brother-in-law, who will fight henceforth for you and with you, even if it be against his own people.

"He does not beg for mercy—he can dare anything! But I am a woman—my heart is soft—I ask for the lives of my husband and my son, who is the grandson of your chief!"

"He is a coward who touches this man!" exclaimed the leader, and a thunder of warwhoops went up in approval of his words.

The warriors formed themselves in two great columns, riding twenty abreast, behind and in front of the strangers. The old chief came out to meet them, and took his son-inlaw's hand. Thus they entered the village in battle array, but with hearts touched with wonder and great gladness, discharging their arrows upward in clouds and singing peace-songs.

II
THE MADNESS OF BALD EAGLE

"It was many years ago, when I was only a child," began White Ghost, the patriarchal old chief of the Yanktonnais Sioux, "that our band was engaged in a desperate battle with the Rees and Mandans. The cause of the fight was a peculiar one. I will tell you about it." And he laid aside his longstemmed pipe and settled himself to the recital.

"At that time the Yanktonnais numbered a little over forty families. We were nicknamed by the other bands Shunkikcheka, or Domestic Dogs, because of our owning large numbers of these animals. My father was the head chief.

"Our favorite wintering place was a timbered tract near the mouth of the Grand River, and it was here that we met the Blackfoot Sioux in the fall hunt. On the opposite side of the river from our camp was the permanent village of the Rees and Mandans, whose houses were of dirt and partly underground. For a hundred years before this time they had planted large gardens, and we were accustomed to buy of them corn, beans, and pumpkins. From time to time our people had made treaties of peace with them. Each family of the Rees had one or two buffalo boats—not round, as the Sioux made them, but two or three skins long. In these boats they brought quantities of dried beans and other vegetables to trade with us for jerked buffalo meat.

"It was a great gathering and a time of general festivity and hospitality. The Sioux young men were courting the Ree girls, and the Ree braves were courting our girls, while the old people bartered their produce. All day the river was alive with canoes and its banks rang with the laughter of the youths and maidens.

"My father's younger brother, whose name was Big Whip, had a close friend, a young man who ever after the event of which I am about to tell you was known as Bald Eagle. They were both daring young men and very ambitious for distinction. They had been following the Ree girls to their canoes as they returned to their homes in the evening.

"Big Whip and his friend stood upon the river bank at sunset, one with a quiver full of arrows upon his back while the other carried a gun under his blanket. Nearly all the people of the other village had crossed the river, and the chief of the Rees, whose name was Bald Eagle, went home with his wife last of all. It was about dusk as they entered their bullhide boat, and the two Sioux stood there looking at them.

"Suddenly Big Whip exclaimed: 'Friend, let us kill the chief. I dare you to kill and scalp him!' His friend replied:

"'It shall be as you say. I will stand by you in all things. I am willing to die with you.'

"Accordingly Bald Eagle pulled out his gun and shot the Ree dead. From that day he took his name. The old man fell backward into his boat, and the old woman screamed and wept as she rowed him across the river. The other young man shot an arrow or two at the wife, but she continued to row until she reached the other bank.

"There was great excitement on both sides of the river as soon as the people saw what had happened. There were two camps of Sioux, the Blackfoot Sioux and the Yanktonnais, or our people. Of course the Mandans and Rees greatly outnumbered us; their camp must have numbered two or three thousand, which was more than we had in our combined camps.

"There was a Sioux whose name was Black Shield, who had intermarried among the Rees. He came down to the opposite bank of the Missouri and shouted to us:

"'Of which one of your bands is the man who killed Bald Eagle?'

"One of the Blackfoot Sioux replied:

"'It is a man of the Yanktonnais Sioux who killed Bald Eagle.'

"Then he said: 'The Rees wish to do battle with them; you had better withdraw from their camp.'

"Accordingly the Blackfeet retired about a mile from us upon the bluffs and pitched their tents, while the Yanktonnais remained on the flats. The two bands had been great rivals in courage and the art of war, so we did not ask for help from our kinsfolk, but during the night we dug trenches about the camp, the inner one for the women and children, and the outer one for the men to stay in and do battle.

"The next morning at daybreak the enemy landed and approached our camp in great numbers. Some of their women and old men came also, and sat upon the bluffs to watch the fight and to carry off their dead and wounded. The Blackfeet likewise were watching the battle from the bluffs,

and just before the fight began one Blackfoot came in with his wife and
joined us. His name was Red Dog's Track, but from that day he was called
He-Came-Back. His wife was a Yanktonnais, and he had said to her: 'If I
don't join your tribe to-day, my brothers-in-law will call me a coward.'

"The Sioux were well entrenched and well armed with guns and arrows,
and their aim was deadly, so that the Rees crawled up gradually and took
every opportunity to pick off any Sioux who ventured to show his head
above the trenches. In like manner every Ree who exposed himself was sure
to die.

"Up to this time no one had seen the two men who made all the trouble.
There was a natural hollow in the bank, concealed by buffalo berry bushes,
very near where they stood when Bald Eagle shot the Ree.

"'Friend,' said Big Whip, 'it is likely that our own people will punish us
for this deed. They will pursue and kill us wherever they find us. They have
the right to do this. The best thing is to drop into this washout and remain
there until they cease to look for us.'

"They did so, and remained hidden during the night. But, after the fight
began, Big Whip said again: 'Friend, we are the cause of the deaths of many
brave men this day. We committed the act to show our bravery. We dared
each other to do it. It will now become us as warriors to join our band.'

"They both stripped, and taking their weapons in hand, ran toward the
camp. They had to pass directly through the enemy's lines, but they were
not recognized till they had fairly passed them. Then they were between
two fires. When they had almost reached the entrenchment they faced
about and fired at the Rees, jumping about incessantly to avoid being hit,
as is the Indian fashion. Bullets and arrows were flying all about them like
hail, but at last they dropped back unhurt into the Sioux trenches. Thus the
two men saved their reputation for bravery, and their people never openly
reproached them for the events of that day. Young men are often rash, but it
is not well to reprove one for a brave deed lest he become a coward.

"Many were killed, but more of the Rees than of our band. About the
middle of the afternoon there came a cold rain. It was in the fall of the year.
The bow-strings were wet, and the guns were only flint-locks. You know

when the flint becomes wet it is useless, and it looked as if the fight must be with knives.

"But the Rees were much disheartened. They had lost many. The women were all the time carrying off the wounded, and there were the Blackfoot Sioux watching them from the hills. They turned and fled toward the river. The Sioux followed like crazy wolves, tomahawking the tired and slow ones. Many were killed at the boats, and some of the boats were punctured with shot and sank. Some carried a load of Sioux arrows back across the river. That was the greatest battle ever fought by our band," the old man concluded, with a deep sigh of mingled satisfaction and regret.

III
THE SINGING SPIRIT

I

"Ho my steed, we must climb one more hill! My reputation depends upon my report!"

Anookasan addressed his pony as if he were a human companion, urged on like himself by human need and human ambition. And yet in his heart he had very little hope of sighting any buffalo in that region at just that time of the year.

The Yankton Sioux were ordinarily the most far-sighted of their people in selecting a winter camp, but this year the late fall had caught them rather far east of the Missouri bottoms, their favorite camping-ground. The upper Jim River, called by the Sioux the River of Gray Woods, was usually bare of large game at that season. Their store of jerked buffalo meat did not hold out as they had hoped, and by March it became an urgent necessity to send out scouts for buffalo.

The old men at the tiyo teepee (council lodge) held a long council. It was decided to select ten of their bravest and hardiest young men to explore the country within three days' journey of their camp.

"Anookasan, uyeyo-o-o, woo, woo!" Thus the ten men were summoned to the council lodge early in the evening to receive their commission. Anookasan was the first called and first to cross the circle of the teepees. A young man of some thirty years, of the original native type, his massive form was wrapped in a fine buffalo robe with the hair inside. He wore a stately eagle feather in his scalp-lock, but no paint about his face.

As he entered the lodge all the inmates greeted him with marked respect, and he was given the place of honor. When all were seated the great drum was struck and a song sung by four deep-chested men. This was the prelude to a peculiar ceremony.

A large red pipe, which had been filled and laid carefully upon the central hearth, was now taken up by an old man, whose face was painted red. First he held it to the ground with the words: "Great Mother, partake of this!" Then he held it toward the sky, saying: "Great Father, smoke this!" Finally he lighted it, took four puffs, pointing it to the four corners of the earth in turn, and lastly presented it to Anookasan. This was the oath of office, administered by the chief of the council lodge. The other nine were similarly commissioned, and all accepted the appointment.

It was no light task that was thus religiously enjoined upon these ten men. It meant at the least several days and nights of wandering in search of signs of the wily buffalo. It was a public duty, and a personal one as well; one that must involve untold hardship; and if overtaken by storm the messengers were in peril of death!

Anookasan returned to his teepee with some misgiving. His old charger, which had so often carried him to victory, was not so strong as he had been in his prime. As his master approached the lodge the old horse welcomed him with a gentle whinny. He was always tethered near by, ready for any emergency.

"Ah, Wakan! we are once more called upon to do duty! We shall set out before daybreak."

As he spoke, he pushed nearer a few strips of the poplar bark, which was oats to the Indian pony of the olden time.

Anookasan had his extra pair of buffaloskin moccasins with the hair inside, and his scanty provision of dried meat neatly done up in a small packet and fastened to his saddle. With his companions he started northward, up the River of the Gray Woods, five on the east side and a like number on the west.

The party had separated each morning, so as to cover as much ground as possible, having agreed to return at night to the river. It was now the third day; their food was all but gone, their steeds much worn, and the signs seemed to indicate a storm. Yet the hunger of their friends and their own pride impelled them to persist, for out of many young men they had been chosen, therefore they must prove themselves equal to the occasion.

The sun, now well toward the western horizon, cast over snow-covered plains a purplish light. No living creature was in sight and the quest seemed hopeless, but Anookasan was not one to accept defeat.

"There may be an outlook from yonder hill which will turn failure into success," he thought, as he dug his heels into the sides of his faithful nag. At the same time he started a "Strong Heart" song to keep his courage up!

At the summit of the ascent he paused and gazed steadily before him. At the foot of the next coteau he beheld a strip of black. He strained his eyes to look, for the sun had already set behind the hilltops. It was a great herd of buffaloes, he thought, which was grazing on the foot-hills.

"Hi hi, uncheedah! Hi, hi, tunkasheedah!" he was about to exclaim in gratitude, when, looking more closely, he discovered his mistake. The dark patch was only timber.

His horse could not carry him any further, so he got off and ran behind him toward the river. At dusk he hailed his companions.

"Ho, what success?" one cried.

"Not a sign of even a lone bull," replied another.

"Yet I saw a gray wolf going north this evening. His direction is propitious," remarked Anookasan, as he led the others down the slope and into the heavy timber. The river just here made a sharp turn, forming a densely wooded semicircle, in the shelter of a high bluff.

The braves were all downhearted because of their ill-luck, and only the sanguine spirit of Anookasan kept them from utter discouragement. Their slight repast had been taken and each man had provided himself with abundance of dry grass and twigs for a bed. They had built a temporary wigwam of the same material, in the center of which there was a generous fire. Each man stretched himself out upon his robe in the glow of it. Anookasan filled the red pipe, and, having lighted it, he took one or two hasty puffs and held it up to the moon, which was scarcely visible behind the cold clouds.

"Great Mother, partake of this smoke! May I eat meat to-morrow!" he exclaimed with solemnity. Having uttered this prayer, he handed the pipe to the man nearest him.

For a time they all smoked in silence; then came a distant call.

"Ah, it is Shunkmanito, the wolf! There is something cheering in his voice to-night," declared Anookasan. "Yes, I am sure he is telling us not to be discouraged. You know that the wolf is one of our best friends in trouble. Many a one has been guided back to his home by him in a blizzard, or led to game when in desperate need. My friends, let us not turn back in the morning; let us go north one more day!"

No one answered immediately, and again silence reigned, while one by one they pulled the reluctant whiffs of smoke through the long stem of the calumet.

"What is that?" said one of the men, and all listened intently to catch the delicate sound. They were familiar with all the noises of the night and voices of the forest, but this was not like any of them.

"It sounds like the song of a mosquito, and one might forget while he listens that this is not midsummer," said one.

"I hear also the medicine-man's single drumbeat," suggested another.

"There is a tradition," remarked Anookasan, that many years ago a party of hunters went up the river on a scout like this of ours. They never returned. Afterward, in the summer, their bones were found near the home of a strange creature, said to be a little man, but he had hair all over him. The Isantees call him Chanotedah. Our old men give him the name Oglugechana. This singular being is said to be no larger than a new-born babe. He speaks an unknown tongue.

"The home of Oglugechana is usually a hollow stump, around which all of the nearest trees are felled by lightning. There is an open spot in the deep woods wherever he dwells. His weapons are the plumes of various birds. Great numbers of these variegated feathers are to be found in the deserted lodge of the little man.

"It is told by the old men that Oglugechana has a weird music by which he sometimes bewitches lone travelers. He leads them hither and thither about his place until they have lost their senses. Then he speaks to them. He may make of them great war-prophets or medicinemen, but his commands are hard to fulfill. If any one sees him and comes away before he is bewildered, the man dies as soon as he smells the camp-fire, or when he enters his home his nearest relative dies suddenly."

The warrior who related this legend assumed the air of one who narrates authentic history, and his listeners appeared to be seriously impressed. What we call the supernatural was as real to them as any part of their lives.

"This thing does not stop to breathe at all. His music seems to go on endlessly," said one, with considerable uneasiness.

"It comes from the heavy timber north of us, under the high cliff," reported a warrior who had stepped outside of the rude temporary structure to inform himself more clearly of the direction of the sound.

"Anookasan, you are our leader—tell us what we should do! We will follow you. I believe we ought to leave this spot immediately. This is perhaps the spirit of some dead enemy," suggested another. Meanwhile, the red pipe was refilled and sent around the circle to calm their disturbed spirits.

When the calumet returned at last to the one addressed, he took it in a preoccupied manner, and spoke between labored pulls on the stem.

"I am just like yourselves—nothing more than flesh—with a spirit that is as ready to leave me as water to run from a punctured water-bag! When we think thus, we are weak. Let us rather think upon the brave deeds of our ancestors! This singing spirit has a gentle voice; I am ready to follow and learn if it be an enemy or no. Let us all be found together next summer if need be!"

"Ho, ho, ho!" was the full-throated response.

"All put on your war-paint," suggested Anookasan. "Have your knives and arrows ready!"

They did so, and all stole silently through the black forest in the direction of the mysterious sound. Clearer and clearer it came through the frosty air; but it was a foreign sound to the savage ear. Now it seemed to them almost like a distant water-fall; then it recalled the low hum of summer insects and the drowsy drone of the bumblebee. Thump, thump, thump! was the regular accompaniment.

Nearer and nearer to the cliff they came, deeper into the wild heart of the woods. At last out of the gray, formless night a dark shape appeared! It looked to them like a huge buffalo bull standing motionless in the forest, and from his throat there apparently proceeded the thump of the medicine drum, and the song of the beguiling spirit!

All of a sudden a spark went up into the air. As they continued to approach, there became visible a deep glow about the middle of the dark object. Whatever it was, they had never heard of anything like it in all their lives!

Anookasan was a little in advance of his companions, and it was he who finally discovered a wall of logs laid one upon another. Half way up there seemed to be stretched a par-fleche (raw-hide), from which a dim light emanated. He still thought of Oglugechana, who dwells within a hollow tree, and determined to surprise and if possible to overpower this wonderworking old man.

All now took their knives in their hands and advanced with their leader to the attack upon the log hut. "Wa-wa-wa-wa, woo, woo!" they cried. Zip, zip! went the par-fleche door and window, and they all rushed in!

There sat a man upon a roughly hewn stool. He was attired in wolfskins and wore a foxskin cap upon his head. The larger portion of his face was clothed with natural fur. A rudely made cedar fiddle was tucked under his furred chin. Supporting it with his left hand, he sawed it vigorously with a bow that was not unlike an Indian boy's miniature weapon, while his moccasined left foot came down upon the sod floor in time with the music. When the shrill war-whoop came, and the door and window were cut in strips by the knives of the Indians, he did not even cease playing, but instinctively he closed his eyes, so as not to behold the horror of his own end.

II

It was long ago, upon the rolling prairie south of the Devil's Lake, that a motley body of hunters gathered near a mighty herd of the bison, in the Moon of Falling Leaves. These were the first generation of the Canadian mixed-bloods, who sprang up in such numbers as to form almost a new people. These semi-wild Americans soon became a necessity to the Hudson Bay Company, as they were the greatest hunters of the bison, and made more use of this wonderful animal than even their aboriginal ancestors.

A curious race of people this, in their make-up and their customs! Their shaggy black hair was allowed to grow long, reaching to their broad shoulders, then cut off abruptly, making their heads look like a thatched house. Their dark faces were in most cases well covered with hair, their teeth large and white, and their eyes usually liquid black, although occasionally one had a tiger-brown or cold-gray eye. Their costume was a buckskin shirt with abundance of fringes, buckskin pantaloons with short leggins, a gay sash, and a cap of fox-fur. Their arms consisted of flint-lock guns, hatchets, and butcher-knives. Their ponies were small, but as hardy as themselves.

As these men gathered in the neighborhood of an immense herd of buffaloes, they busied themselves in adjusting the girths of their beautifully beaded pillow-like saddles. Among them there were exceptional riders and hunters. It was said that few could equal Antoine Michaud in feats of riding into and through the herd. There he stood, all alone, the observed of many others. It was his habit to give several Indian yells when the onset began, so as to insure a successful hunt.

In this instance, Antoine gave his usual whoops, and when they had almost reached the herd, he lifted his flint-lock over his head and plunged into the black moving mass. With a sound like the distant rumbling of thunder, those tens of thousands of buffalo hoofs were pounding the earth in retreat. Thus Antoine disappeared!

His wild steed dashed into the midst of the vast herd. Fortunately for him, the animals kept clear of him; but alas! the gap through which he had entered instantly closed again.

He yelled frantically to secure an outlet, but without effect. He had tied a red bandanna around his head to keep the hair off his face, and he now took this off and swung it crazily about him to scatter the buffalo, but it availed him nothing.

With such a mighty herd in flight, the speed could not be great; therefore the "Bois Brule" settled himself to the situation, allowing his pony to canter along slowly to save his strength. It required much tact and presence of mind to keep an open space, for the few paces of obstruction behind had gradually grown into a mile.

The mighty host moved continually southward, walking and running alternately. As the sun neared the western horizon, it fired the sky above them, and all the distant hills and prairies were in the glow of it, but immediately about them was a thick cloud of dust, and the ground appeared like a fire-swept plain.

Suddenly Antoine was aware of a tremendous push from behind. The animals smelled the cool water of a spring which formed a large bog in the midst of the plain. This solitary pond or marsh was a watering-place for the wild animals. All pushed and edged toward it; it was impossible for any one to withstand the combined strength of so many.

Antoine and his steed were in imminent danger of being pushed into the mire and trampled upon, but a mere chance brought them upon solid ground. As they were crowded across the marsh, his pony drank heartily, and he, for the first time, let go his bridle, put his two palms together for a dipper, and drank greedily of the bitter water. He had not eaten since early morning, so he now pulled up some bulrushes and ate of the tender bulbs, while the pony grazed as best he could on the tops of the tall grass.

It was now dark. The night was wellnigh intolerable for Antoine. The buffalo were about him in countless numbers, regarding him with vicious glances. It was only by reason of the natural offensiveness of man that they gave him any space. The bellowing of the bulls became general, and there was a marked uneasiness on the part of the herd. This was a sign of approaching storm, therefore the unfortunate hunter had this additional cause for anxiety. Upon the western horizon were seen some flashes of lightning.

The cloud which had been a mere speck upon the horizon had now increased to large proportions. Suddenly the wind came, and lightning flashes became more frequent, showing the ungainly forms of the animals like strange monsters in the white light. The colossal herd was again in violent motion. It was a blind rush for shelter, and no heed was paid to buffalo wallows or even deep gulches. All was in the deepest of darkness. There seemed to be groaning in heaven and earth—millions of hoofs and throats roaring in unison!

As a shipwrecked man clings to a mere fragment of wood, so Antoine, although almost exhausted with fatigue, still stuck to the back of his equally plucky pony. Death was imminent for them both. As the mad rush continued, every flash displayed heaps of bison in death struggle under the hoofs of their companions.

From time to time Antoine crossed himself and whispered a prayer to the Virgin; and again he spoke to his horse after the fashion of an Indian:

"Be brave, be strong, my horse! If we survive this trial, you shall have great honor!"

The stampede continued until they reached the bottom lands, and, like a rushing stream, their course was turned aside by the steep bank of a creek or small river. Then they moved more slowly in wide sweeps or circles, until the storm ceased, and the exhausted hunter, still in his saddle, took some snatches of sleep.

When he awoke and looked about him again it was morning. The herd had entered the strip of timber which lay on both sides of the river, and it was here that Antoine conceived his first distinct hope of saving himself.

"Waw, waw, waw!" was the hoarse cry that came to his ears, apparently from a human being in distress. Antoine strained his eyes and craned his neck to see who it could be. Through an opening in the branches ahead he perceived a large grizzly bear, lying along an inclined limb and hugging it desperately to maintain his position. The herd had now thoroughly pervaded the timber, and the bear was likewise hemmed in. He had taken to his unaccustomed refuge after making a brave stand against several bulls, one of which lay dead near by, while he himself was bleeding from many wounds.

Antoine had been assiduously looking for a friendly tree, by means of which he hoped to effect his escape from captivity by the army of bison. His horse, by chance, made his way directly under the very box-elder that was sustaining the bear and there was a convenient branch just within his reach. The Bois Brule was not then in an aggressive mood, and he saw at a glance that the occupant of the tree would not interfere with him. They were, in fact, companions in distress. Antoine tried to give a war-whoop as he sprang desperately from the pony's back and seized the cross limb with both his hands.

The hunter dangled in the air for a minute that to him seemed a year. Then he gathered up all the strength that was in him, and with one grand effort he pulled himself up on the limb.

If he had failed in this, he would have fallen to the ground under the hoofs of the buffaloes, and at their mercy.

After he had adjusted his seat as comfortably as he could, Antoine surveyed the situation. He had at least escaped from sudden and certain death. It grieved him that he had been forced to abandon his horse, and he had no idea how far he had come nor any means of returning to his friends, who had, no doubt, given him up for lost. His immediate needs were rest and food.

Accordingly he selected a fat cow and emptied into her sides one barrel of his gun, which had been slung across his chest. He went on shooting until he had killed many fat cows, greatly to the discomfiture of his neighbor, the bear, while the bison vainly struggled among themselves to keep the fatal spot clear.

By the middle of the afternoon the main body of the herd had passed, and Antoine was sure that his captivity had at last come to an end. Then he swung himself from his limb to the ground, and walked stiffly to the carcass of the nearest cow, which he dressed and prepared himself a meal. But first he took a piece of liver on a long pole to the bear!

Antoine finally decided to settle in the recesses of the heavy timber for the winter, as he was on foot and alone, and not able to travel any great distance. He jerked the meat of all the animals he had killed, and prepared their skins for bedding and clothing. The Bois Brule and Ami, as he called the bear, soon became necessary to one another. The former considered the bear very good company, and the latter had learned that man's business, after all, is not to kill every animal he meets. He had been fed and kindly treated, when helpless from his wounds, and this he could not forget.

Antoine was soon busy erecting a small log hut, while the other partner kept a sharp lookout, and, after his hurts were healed, often brought in some small game. The two had a perfect understanding without many words; at least, the speech was all upon one side! In his leisure moments Antoine had occupied himself with whittling out a rude fiddle of cedar-wood, strung with the guts of a wild cat that he had killed. Every evening that winter he would sit down after supper and play all the old familiar pieces, varied with improvisations of his own. At first, the music and the incessant pounding time with his foot annoyed the bear. At times, too, the Canadian would call out the figures for the dance. All this Ami became accustomed to in time, and even showed no small interest in the buzzing of the little cedar box. Not infrequently, he was out in the evening, and the human partner was left alone. It chanced, quite fortunately, that the bear was absent on the night that the red folk rudely invaded the lonely hut.

The calmness of the strange being had stayed their hands. They had never before seen a man of other race than their own!

"Is this Chanotedah? Is he man, or beast?" the warriors asked one another.

"Ho, wake up, koda!" exclaimed Anookasan. "Maybe he is of the porcupine tribe, ashamed to look at us!"

At this moment they spied the haunch of venison which swung from a cross-stick over a fine bed of coals, in front of the rude mud chimney.

"Ho, koda has something to eat! Sit down, sit down!" they shouted to one another.

Now Antoine opened his eyes for the first time upon his unlooked-for guests. They were a haggard and hungry-looking set. Anookasan extended his hand, and Antoine gave it a hearty shake. He set his fiddle against the wall and began to cut up the smoking venison into generous pieces and place it before them. All ate like famished men, while the firelight intensified the red paint upon their wild and warlike faces.

When he had satisfied his first hunger, Anookasan spoke in signs. "Friend, we have never before heard a song like that of your little cedar box! We had supposed it to be a spirit, or some harmful thing, hence our attack upon it. We never saw any people of your sort. What is your tribe?"

Antoine explained his plight in the same manner, and the two soon came to an understanding. The Canadian told the starving hunters of a buffalo herd a little way to the north, and one of their number was dispatched homeward with the news. In two days the entire band reached Antoine's place. The Bois Brule was treated with kindness and honor, and the tribe gave him a wife. Suffice it to say that Antoine lived and died among the Yanktons at a good old age; but Ami could not brook the invasion upon their hermit life. He was never seen after that first evening.

IV
THE FAMINE

On the Assiniboine River in western Manitoba there stands an old, historic trading-post, whose crumbling walls crown a high promontory in the angle formed by its junction with a tributary stream. This is Fort Ellis, a mistress of the wilderness and lodestone of savage tribes between the years 1830 and 1870.

Hither at that early day the Indians brought their buffalo robes and beaver skins to exchange for merchandise, ammunition, and the "spirit water." Among the others there presently appeared a band of renegade Sioux—the exiles, as they called themselves—under White Lodge, whose father, Little Crow, had been a leader in the outbreak of 1862. Now the great warchief was dead, and his people were prisoners or fugitives. The shrewd Scotch trader, McLeod, soon discovered that the Sioux were skilled hunters, and therefore he exerted himself to befriend them, as well as to encourage a feeling of good will between them and the Canadian tribes who were accustomed to make the old fort their summer rendezvous.

Now the autumn had come, after a long summer of feasts and dances, and the three tribes broke up and dispersed as usual in various directions. White Lodge had twin daughters, very handsome, whose ears had been kept burning with the proposals of many suitors, but none had received any definite encouragement. There were one or two who would have been quite willing to forsake their own tribes and follow the exiles had they not feared too much the ridicule of the braves. Even Angus McLeod, the trader's eldest son, had need of all his patience and caution, for he had never seen any woman he admired so much as the piquant Magaskawee, called The Swan, one of these belles of the forest.

The Sioux journeyed northward, toward the Mouse River. They had wintered on that stream before, and it was then the feeding ground of large herds of buffalo. When it was discovered that the herds were moving westward, across the Missouri, there was no little apprehension. The shrewd medicine-man became aware of the situation, and hastened to announce his prophecy:

"The Great Mystery has appeared to me in a dream! He showed me men with haggard and thin faces. I interpret this to mean a scarcity of food during the winter."

The chief called his counselors together and set before them the dream of the priest, whose prophecy, he said, was already being fulfilled in part by the westward movement of the buffalo. It was agreed that they should lay up all the dried meat they could obtain; but even for this they were too late. The storms were already at hand, and that winter was more severe than any that the old men could recall in their traditions. The braves killed all the small game for a wide circuit around the camp, but the buffalo had now crossed the river, and that country was not favorable for deer. The more enterprising young men organized hunting expeditions to various parts of the open prairie, but each time they returned with empty hands.

The "Moon of Sore Eyes," or March, had come at last, and Wazeah, the God of Storm, was still angry. Their scant provision of dried meat had held out wonderfully, but it was now all but consumed. The Sioux had but little ammunition, and the snow was still so deep that it was impossible for them to move away to any other region in search of game. The worst was feared; indeed, some of the children and feeble old people had already succumbed.

White Lodge again called his men together in council, and it was determined to send a messenger to Fort Ellis to ask for relief. A young man called Face-the-Wind was chosen for his exceptional qualities of speed and endurance upon long journeys. The old medicine-man, whose shrewd prophecy had gained for him the confidence of the people, now came forward. He had closely observed the appearance of the messenger selected, and had taken note of the storm and distance. Accordingly he said:

"My children, the Great Mystery is offended, and this is the cause of all our suffering! I see a shadow hanging over our messenger, but I will pray to the Great Spirit—perhaps he may yet save him!—Great Mystery, be thou merciful! Strengthen this young man for his journey, that he may be able to finish it and to send us aid! If we see the sun of summer again, we will offer the choicest of our meats to thee, and do thee great honor!"

During this invocation, as occasionally happens in March, a loud peal of thunder was heard. This coincidence threw the prophet almost into a frenzy, and the poor people were all of a tremble. Face-the-Wind believed that the prayer was directly answered, and though weakened by fasting and unfit for the task before him, he was encouraged to make the attempt.

He set out on the following day at dawn, and on the third day staggered into the fort, looking like a specter and almost frightening the people. He was taken to McLeod's house and given good care. The poor fellow, delirious with hunger, fancied himself engaged in mortal combat with Eyah, the god of famine, who has a mouth extending from ear to ear. Wherever he goes there is famine, for he swallows all that he sees, even whole nations!

The legend has it that Eyah fears nothing but the jingling of metal: so finally the dying man looked up into McLeod's face and cried: "Ring your bell in his face, Wahadah!"

The kind-hearted factor could not refuse, and as the great bell used to mark the hours of work and of meals pealed out untimely upon the frosty air, the Indian started up and in that moment breathed his last. He had given no news, and McLeod and his sons could only guess at the state of affairs upon the Mouse River.

While the men were in council with her father, Magaskawee had turned over the contents of her work-bag. She had found a small roll of birch-bark in which she kept her porcupine quills for embroidery, and pulled the delicate layers apart. The White Swan was not altogether the untutored Indian maiden, for she had lived in the family of a missionary in the States, and had learned both to speak and write some English. There was no ink, no pen or pencil, but with her bone awl she pressed upon the white side of the bark the following words:

MR. ANGUS McLEOD:—

We are near the hollow rock on the Mouse River. The buffalo went away across the Missouri, and our powder and shot are gone. We are starving. Good-bye, if I don't see you again.

MAGASKAWEE.

The girl entrusted this little note to her grandmother, and she in turn gave it to the messenger. But he, as we know, was unable to deliver it.

"Angus, tell the boys to bury the poor fellow to-morrow. I dare say he brought us some news from White Lodge, but we have got to go to the happy hunting-grounds to get it, or wait till the exile band returns in the spring. Evidently," continued McLeod, "he fell sick on the way: or else he was starving!"

This last suggestion horrified Angus. "I believe, father," he exclaimed, "that we ought to examine his bundle."

A small oblong packet was brought forth from the dead man's belt and carefully unrolled.

There were several pairs of moccasins, and within one of these Angus found something wrapped up nicely. He proceeded to unwind the long strings of deerskin with which it was securely tied, and brought forth a thin sheet of birch-bark. At first, there seemed to be nothing more, but a closer scrutiny revealed the impression of the awl, and the bit of nature's parchment was brought nearer to his face, and scanned with a zeal equal to that of any student of ancient hieroglyphics.

"This tells the whole story, father!" exclaimed the young man at last. "Magaskawee's note—just listen!" and he read it aloud. "I shall start to-morrow. We can take enough provision and ammunition on two sleds, with six dogs to each. I shall want three good men to go with me." Angus spoke with decision.

"Well, we can't afford to lose our best hunters; and you might also bring home with you what furs and robes they have on hand," was his father's prudent reply.

"I don't care particularly for the skins," Angus declared; but he at once began hurried preparations for departure.

In the meantime affairs grew daily more desperate in the exile village on the far-away Mouse River, and a sort of Indian hopelessness and resignation settled down upon the little community. There were few who really expected their messenger to reach the fort, or believed that even if he did so, relief would be sent in time to save them. White Lodge, the father of his people, was determined to share with them the last mouthful of food, and every morning Winona and Magaskawee went with scanty portions in their hands to those whose supply had entirely failed.

On the outskirts of the camp there dwelt an old woman with an orphan grandchild, who had been denying herself for some time in order that the child might live longer. This poor teepee the girls visited often, and one on each side they raised the exhausted woman and poured into her mouth the warm broth they had brought with them.

It was on the very day Face-the-Wind reached Fort Ellis that a young hunter who had ventured further from the camp than any one else had the luck to bring down a solitary deer with his bow and arrow. In his weakness he had reached camp very late, bearing the deer with the utmost difficulty upon his shoulders. It was instantly separated into as many pieces as there were lodges of the famishing Sioux. These delicious morsels were hastily cooked and eagerly devoured, but among so many there was scarcely more than a mouthful to the share of each, and the brave youth himself did not receive enough to appease in the least his craving!

On the eve of Angus' departure for the exile village, Three Stars, a devoted suitor of Winona's, accompanied by another Assiniboine brave, appeared unexpectedly at the fort. He at once asked permission to join the relief party, and they set out at daybreak.

The lead-dog was the old reliable Mack, who had been in service for several seasons on winter trips. All of the white men were clad in buckskin shirts and pantaloons, with long fringes down the sides, fur caps and fur-lined moccasins. Their guns were fastened to the long, toboggan-like sleds.

The snow had thawed a little and formed an icy crust, and over this fresh snow had fallen, which a northwest wind swept over the surface like ashes after a prairie fire. The sun appeared for a little time in the morning, but it seemed as if he were cutting short his course on account of the bleak day, and had protected himself with pale rings of fire.

The dogs laid back their ears, drew in their tails, and struck into their customary trot, but even old Mack looked back frequently, as if reluctant to face such a pricking and scarifying wind. The men felt the cold still more keenly, although they had taken care to cover every bit of the face except one eye, and that was completely blinded at times by the granulated snow.

The sun early retreated behind a wall of cloud, and the wind moaned and wailed like a living creature in anguish. At last they approached the creek where they had planned to camp for the night. There was nothing to be seen but a few stunted willows half buried in the drifts, but the banks of the little stream afforded some protection from the wind.

"Whoa!" shouted the leader, and the dogs all stopped, sitting down on their haunches. "Come, Mack!" (with a wave of the hand), "lead your fellows down to the creek!"

The old dog started down at the word, and all the rest followed. A space was quickly cleared of snow, while one man scoured the thickets in search of brush for fuel. In a few minutes the tent was up and a fire kindled in the center, while the floor was thickly strewn with twigs of willow, over which buffalo robes were spread. Three Stars attended to supper, and soon in the midst of the snapping willow fire a kettle was boiling. All partook of strong tea, dried meat of buffalo, and pemmican, a mixture of pounded dried meat with wild cherries and melted fat. The dogs, to whom one-half the tent was assigned, enjoyed a hearty meal and fell into a deep sleep, lying one against another.

After supper Jerry drove two sticks into the ground, one on each side of the fire, and connected the two by a third one over the blaze. Upon this all hung their socks to dry—most of them merely square pieces of blanket cut to serve that purpose. Soon each man rolled himself in his own buffalo robe and fell asleep.

All night the wind raged. The lonely teepee now and then shuddered violently, as a stronger blast than usual almost lifted it from the ground. No one stirred except from time to time one of the dogs, who got up snarling and sniffing the cold air, turned himself round several times as if on a pivot, and finally lay down for another nap.

In the morning the travelers one by one raised their heads and looked through the smoke-hole, then fell back again with a grunt. All the world appeared without form and void. Presently, however, the light of the sun was seen as if through a painted window, and by afternoon they were able to go on, the wind having partially subsided. This was only a taste of the weather encountered by the party on their unseasonable trip; but had it been ten times harder, it would never have occurred to Angus to turn back.

On the third day the rescuers approached the camp of the exiles. There was an ominous quiet; no creature was to be seen; but the smoke which ascended into the air in perpendicular columns assured them that some, at least, were still alive. The party happened to reach first the teepee of the poor old woman who had been so faithfully ministered to by the twin sisters. They had no longer any food to give, but they had come to build her fire, if she should have survived the night. At the very door of the lodge they heard the jingle of dog-bells, but they had not time to announce the joyful news before the men were in sight.

In another minute Angus and Three Stars were beside them, holding their wasted hands.

V
THE CHIEF SOLDIER

Just outside of a fine large wigwam of smoke-tanned buffalo-skins stood Tawasuota, very early upon an August morning of the year 1862. Behind the wigwam there might have been seen a thrifty patch of growing maize, whose tall, graceful stalks resembled as many warriors in dancing-dresses and tasseled head-gear.

"Thanks be to the 'Great Mystery,' I have been successful in the fortunes of war! None can say that Tawasuota is a coward. I have done well; so well that our chief, Little Crow, has offered me the honored position of his chief soldier, ta akich-itah!" he said to himself with satisfaction.

The sun was just over the eastem bank of the Minnesota River, and he could distinctly see upon the level prairie the dwellings of logs which had sprung up there during the year, since Little Crow's last treaty with the whites. "Ugh! they are taking from us our beautiful and game-teeming country!" was his thought as he gazed upon them.

At that moment, out of the conical white teepee, in shape like a new-born mushroom, there burst two little frisky boys, leaping and whooping. They were clad gracefully in garments of fine deerskin, and each wore a miniature feather upon his head, marking them as children of a distinguished warrior.

They danced nimbly around their father, while he stood with all the dignity of a buck elk, viewing the landscape reddened by sunrise and the dwellers therein, the old and the new, the red and the white. He noticed that they were still unmingled; the river divided them.

At last he took the dancing little embryo warriors one in either hand, and lifted them to his majestic shoulders. There he placed them in perfect poise. His haughty spirit found a moment's happiness in fatherhood.

Suddenly Tawasuota set the two boys on the ground again, and signed to them to enter the teepee. Apparently all was quiet. The camps and villages of the Minnesota reservation were undisturbed, so far as he could see, save by the awakening of nature; and the early risers among his people moved about in seeming security, while the smoke of their morning fires arose one by one into the blue. Still the warrior gazed steadily westward, up the river, whence his quick ear had caught the faint but ominous sound of a distant war-whoop.

The ridge beyond the Wahpeton village bounded the view, and between this point and his own village were the agency buildings and the traders' stores. The Indian's keen eye swept the horizon, and finally alighted once more upon the home of his new neighbor across the river, the flaxen-haired white man with many children, who with his white squaw and his little ones worked from sunrise to sunset, much like the beaver family.

Ah! the distant war-whoop once more saluted his ear, but this time nearer and more distinct.

"What! the Rice Creek band is coming in full war-paint! Can it be another Ojibway attack? Ugh, ugh! I will show their warriors again this day what it is to fight!" he exclaimed aloud.

The white traders and Government employees, those of them who were up and about, heard and saw the advancing column of warriors. Yet they showed no sign of anxiety or fear. Most of them thought that there might be some report of Ojibways coming to attack the Sioux,—a not uncommon incident,—and that those warriors were on their way to the post to replenish their powder-horns. A few of the younger men were delighted with the prospect of witnessing an Indian fight.

On swept the armed band, in numbers increasing at every village.

It was true that there had been a growing feeling of distrust among the Indians, because their annuities had been withheld for a long time, and the money payments had been delayed again and again. There were many in great need. The traders had given them credit to some extent (charging them four times the value of the article purchased), and had likewise induced Little Crow to sign over to them ninety-eight thousand dollars, the purchase-price of that part of their reservation lying north of the Minnesota, and already occupied by the whites.

This act had made the chief very unpopular, and he was ready for a desperate venture to regain his influence. Certain warriors among the upper bands of Sioux had even threatened his life, but no one spoke openly of a break with the whites.

When, therefore, the news came to Little Crow that some roving hunters of the Rice Creek band had killed in a brawl two families of white settlers, he saw his opportunity to show once for all to the disaffected that he had no love for the white man. Immediately he sprang upon his white horse, and prepared to make their cause a general one among his people.

Tawasuota had scarcely finished his hasty preparations for war, by painting his face and seeing to the loading of his gun, when he heard the voice of Little Crow outside his lodge.

"You are now my head soldier," said the chief, "and this is your first duty. Little Six and his band have inaugurated the war against the whites. They have already wiped out two families, and are now on their way to the agency. Let my chief soldier fire the first shot.

"Those Indians who have cut their hair and donned the white man's clothing may give the warning; so make haste! If you fall to-day, there is no better day on which to die, and the women of our tribe will weep proud tears for Tawasuota. I leave it with you to lead my warriors." With these words the wily chief galloped away to meet the war-party.

"Here comes Little Crow, the friend of the white man!" exclaimed a warrior, as he approached.

"Friends and warriors, you will learn to-day who are the friends of the white man, and none will dare again to insinuate that I have been against the interests of my own people," he replied.

After a brief consultation with the chiefs he advised the traders:

"Do not hesitate to fill the powder-horns of my warriors; they may be compelled to fight all day."

Soon loud yells were heard along the road to the Indian village.

"Ho, ho! Tawasuota u ye do!" ("He is coming; he is coming!") shouted the warriors in chorus.

The famous war-chief dismounted in silence, gun in hand, and walked directly toward the larger store.

"Friend," he exclaimed, "we may both meet the 'Great Mystery' to-day, but you must go first."

There was a loud report, and the unsuspecting white man lay dead. It was James Lynd, one of the early traders, and a good friend to the Indians.

No sooner had Tawasuota fired the fatal shot than every other Indian discharged his piece. Hither and thither ran the frantic people, seeking safety, but seeking it in vain. They were wholly unprepared and at the mercy of the foe.

The friendly Indians, too, were taken entirely by surprise. They had often heard wild talk of revolt, but it had never had the indorsement of intelligent chiefs, or of such a number as to carry any weight to their minds. Christian Indians rushed in every direction to save, if possible, at least the wives and children of the Government employees. Meanwhile, the new white settlements along the Minnesota River were utterly unconscious of any danger. Not a soul dreamed of the terrible calamity that each passing moment was bringing nearer and nearer.

Tawasuota stepped aside, and took up his pipe. He seemed almost oblivious of what he had done. While the massacre still raged about him in all its awful cruelty, he sat smoking and trying to think collectedly, but his mind was confused, and in his secret thoughts he rebelled against Little Crow. It was a cowardly deed that he had been ordered to commit, he thought; for he had won his reputation solely by brave deeds in battle, and this was more like murdering one of his own tribesmen—this killing of an unarmed white man. Up to this time the killing of a white man was not counted the deed of a warrior; it was murder.

The lesser braves might now satisfy their spite against the traders to their hearts' content, but Tawasuota had been upon the best of terms with all of them.

Suddenly a ringing shout was heard. The chief soldier looked up, and beheld a white man, nearly nude, leap from the roof of the larger store and alight upon the ground hard by him.

He had emptied one barrel of his gun, and, if he chose to do so, could have killed Myrick then and there; but he made no move, exclaiming:

"Ho, ho! Nina iyaye!" ("Run, run!")

Away sped the white man in the direction of the woods and the river.

"Ah, he is swift; he will save himself," thought Tawasuota.

All the Indians had now spied the fugitive; they yelled and fired at him again and again, as if they were shooting at a running deer; but he only ran faster. Just as he had reached the very edge of the sheltering timber a single shot rang out, and he fell headlong.

A loud war-whoop went up, for many believed that this was one of the men who had stolen their trust funds.

Tawasuota continued to sit and smoke in the shade while the carnage and plunder that he had set on foot proceeded on all sides of him. Presently men began to form small parties to cross the river on their mission of death, but he refused to join any of them. At last, several of the older warriors came up to smoke with him.

"Ho, nephew," said one of them with much gravity, "you have precipitated a dreadful calamity. This means the loss of our country, the destruction of our nation. What were you thinking of?"

It was the Wahpeton chief who spoke, a blood-relation to Tawasuota. He did not at once reply, but filled his pipe in silence, and handed it to the man who thus reproached him. It was a just rebuke; for he was a brave man, and he could have refused the request of his chief to open the massacre.

At this moment it was announced that a body of white soldiers were on the march from Fort Ridgeley. A large body of warriors set out to meet them.

"Nephew, you have spilled the first blood of the white man; go, join in battle with the soldiers. They are armed; they can defend themselves," remarked the old chief, and Tawasuota replied:

"Uncle, you speak truth; I have committed the act of a coward. It was not of my own will I did it; nevertheless, I have raised my weapon, and I will fight the whites as long as I live. If I am ever taken, they will first have to kill me." He arose, took up his gun, and joined the war-party.

The dreadful day of massacre was almost ended. The terrified Sioux women and children had fled up the river before the approaching troops. Long shafts of light from the setting sun painted every hill; one side red as with blood, the other dark as the shadow of death. A cloud of smoke from burning homes hung over the beautiful river. Even the permanent dwellings of the Indians were empty, and all the teepees which had dotted with their white cones the west bank of the Minnesota had disappeared. Here and there were small groups of warriors returning from their bloody work, and among them was Tawasuota.

He looked long at the spot where his home had stood; but it was gone, and with it his family. Ah, the beautiful country of his ancestors! he must depart from it forever, for he knew now that the white man would occupy that land. Sadly he sang the spirit-song, and made his appeal to the "Great Mystery," excusing himself by the plea that what he had done had been in the path of duty. There was no glory in it for him; he could wear no eagle feather, nor could he ever recount the deed. It was dreadful to him—the thought that he had fired upon an unarmed and helpless man.

The chief soldier followed the broad trail of the fleeing host, and after some hours he came upon a camp. There were no war-songs nor dances there, as was their wont after a battle, but a strange stillness reigned. Even the dogs scarcely barked at his approach; everything seemed conscious of the awful carnage of the day.

He stopped at a tent and inquired after his beautiful wife and two little sons, whom he had already trained to uphold their father's reputation, but was directed to his mother's teepee.

"Ah, my son, my son, what have you done?" cried his old mother when she saw him. "Come in, come in; let us eat together once more; for I have a foreboding that it is for the last time. Alas, what have you done?"

Tawasuota silently entered the tent of his widowed mother, and his three sisters gave him the place of honor.

"Mother, it is not right to blame our brother," said the eldest. "He was the chief's head soldier; and if he had disobeyed his orders, he would have been called a coward. That he could not bear."

Food was handed him, and he swallowed a few mouthfuls, and gave back the dish.

"You have not yet told me where she is, and the children," he said with a deep sigh.

"My son, my son, I have not, because it will give you pain. I wanted you to eat first! She has been taken away by her own mother to Faribault, among the white people. I could not persuade them to wait until you came. Her people are lovers of the whites. They have even accepted their religion," grieved the good old mother.

Tawasuota's head dropped upon his chest, and he sat silent for a long time. The mother and three sisters were also silent, for they knew how heavy his grief must be. At last he spoke.

"Mother, I am too proud to desert the tribe now and join my wife among the white people. My brother-in-law may lie in my behalf, and say that my hands are not stained with blood; but the spirits of those who died to-day would rebuke me, and the rebuke would be just. No, I must fight the whites until I die; and neither have I fought without cause; but I must see my sons once more before I go."

When Tawasuota left his mother's teepee he walked fast across the circle toward the council lodge to see Little Crow. He drew his blanket closely about him, with his gun underneath. The keen eye of the wily chief detected the severe expression upon the face of his guest, and he hastened to speak first.

"There are times in the life of every great man when he must face hardship and put self aside for the good of his people. You have done well to-day!"

"I care little for myself," replied Tawasuota, "but my heart is heavy to-night. My wife and two boys have been taken away among the whites by my mother-in-law. I fear for their safety, when it is known what we have done."

"Ugh, that old woman is too hasty in accepting the ways of the stranger people!" exclaimed the chief.

"I am now on my way to see them," declared Tawasuota.

"Ugh, ugh, I shall need you to-morrow! My plan is to attack the soldiers at Fort Ridgeley with a strong force. There are not many. Then we shall attack New Ulm and other towns. We will drive them all back into Saint Paul and Fort Snelling." Little Crow spoke with energy.

"You must stay," he added, "and lead the attack either at the fort or at New Ulm."

For some minutes the chief soldier sat in silence.

At last he said simply, "I will do it."

On the following day the attack was made, but it was unsuccessful. The whole State was now alarmed, and all the frontier settlers left alive had flocked to the larger and more protected towns. It had also developed during the day that there was a large party of Sioux who were ready to surrender, thereby showing that they had not been party to the massacre nor indorsed the hasty action of the tribe.

At evening Tawasuota saw that there would be a long war with the whites, and that the Indians must remove their families out of danger. The feeling against all Indians was great. Night had brought him no relief of mind, but it promised to shield him in a hazardous undertaking. He consulted no one, but set out for the distant village of Faribault.

He kept to the flats back of the Minnesota, away from the well-traveled roads, and moved on at a good gait, for he realized that he had to cover a hundred miles in as few hours as possible. Every day that passed would make it more difficult for him to rejoin his family.

Although he kept as far as he could from the settlements, he would come now and then upon a solitary frame house, razed to the ground by the war-parties of the day before. The members of the ill-fated family were to be seen scattered in and about the place; and their white, upturned faces told him that his race must pay for the deed.

The dog that howled pitifully over the dead was often the only survivor of the farmer's household.

Occasionally Tawasuota heard at a distance the wagons of the fugitives, loaded with women and children, while armed men walked before and behind. These caravans were usually drawn by oxen and moved slowly toward some large town.

When the dawn appeared in the east, the chief soldier was compelled to conceal himself in a secluded place. He rolled up in his blanket, lay down in a dry creek-bed among the red willows and immediately fell asleep.

With the next evening he resumed his journey, and reached Faribault toward midnight. Even here every approach was guarded against the possibility of an Indian attack. But there was much forest, and he knew the country well. He reconnoitred, and soon found the Indian community, but dared not approach and enter, for these Indians had allied themselves with the whites; they would be charged with treachery if it were known that they had received a hostile Sioux, and none were so hated by the white people as Little Crow and his war-chief.

He chose a concealed position from which he might watch the movements of his wife, if she were indeed there, and had not been waylaid and slain on the journey hither.

That night was the hardest one that the warrior had ever known. If he slept, it was only to dream of the war-whoop and attack; but at last he found himself broad awake, the sun well up, and yes! there were his two little sons, playing outside their teepee as of old. The next moment he heard the voice of his wife from the deep woods wailing for her husband!

"Oh, take us, husband, take us with you! let us all die together!" she pleaded as she clung to him whom she had regarded as already dead; for she knew of the price that had been put upon his head, and that some of the halfbreeds loved money better than the blood of their Indian mothers.

Tawasuota stood for a minute without speaking, while his huge frame trembled like a mighty pine beneath the thunderbolt.

"No," he said at last. "I shall go, but you must remain. You are a woman, and the white people need not know that your little boys are mine. Bring them here to me this evening that I may kiss them farewell."

The sun was hovering among the treetops when they met again.

"Atay! atay!" ("Papa, papa!") the little fellows cried out in spite of her cautions; but the mother put her finger to her lips, and they became silent. Tawasuota took each boy in his arms, and held him close for a few moments; he smiled to them, but large tears rolled down his cheeks. Then he disappeared in the shadows, and they never saw him again.

The chief soldier lived and died a warrior and an enemy to the white man; but one of his two sons became in after-years a minister of the Christian gospel, under the "Long-Haired Praying Man," Bishop Whipple, of Minnesota.

VI
THE WHITE MAN'S ERRAND

Upon the wide tableland that lies at the back of a certain Indian agency, a camp of a thousand teepees was pitched in a circle, according to the ancient usage. In the center of the circle stood the council lodge, where there were gathered together of an afternoon all the men of years and distinction, some in blankets, some in uniform, and still others clad in beggarly white man's clothing. But the minds of all were alike upon the days of their youth and freedom.

Around the council fire they passed and repassed the pipe of peace, and when the big drum was struck they sang the accompaniment with sad yet pleasant thoughts of the life that is past. Between the songs stories of brave deeds and dangerous exploits were related by the actors in turn, with as much spirit and zest as if they were still living in those days.

"Tum, tum, tum," the drum was sounded.

"Oow, oow!" they hooted in a joyous chorus at the close of each refrain.

"Ho!" exclaimed finally the master of ceremonies for the evening. "It is Zuyamani's story of his great ride that we should now hear! It was not far from this place, upon the Missouri River, and within the recollection of many of us that this occurred. Ye young men must hear!"

"Ho, ho!" was the ready response of all present, and the drum was struck once according to custom. The pipe was filled and handed to Zuyamani, who gravely smoked for a few moments in silence. Then he related his contribution to the unwritten history of our frontier in these words:

"It was during the winter following that summer in which General Sibley pursued many of our people across the Muddy River (1863), that we Hunkpatees, friendly Sioux, were camping at a place called 'Hunt-the-Deer,' about two miles from Fort Rice, Dakota Territory.

"The Chief Soldier of the garrison called one day upon the leading chiefs of our band. To each one he said: 'Lend me your bravest warrior!' Each chief called his principal warriors together and laid the matter before them.

"'The Chief Soldier at this place,' they explained, 'wants to send a message to Fort Berthold, where the Rees and Mandans live, to another Chief Soldier there. The soldiers of the Great Father do not know the way, neither could any of them get through the lines. He asks for a brave man to carry his message.'

"The Mandans and the Rees were our hereditary enemies, but this was not the principal reason for our hesitation. We had declared allegiance to the Great Father at Washington; we had taken our stand against the fighting men of our own nation, and the hostile Sioux were worse than enemies to us at this time!

"Each chief had only called on his leading warriors, and each in turn reported his failure to secure a volunteer.

"Then the Chief Soldier sent again and said: 'Is there not a young man among you who dares to face death? If he reaches the fort with my message, he will need to be quick-witted as well as brave, and the Great Father will not forget him!'

"Now all the chiefs together called all the young men in a great council, and submitted to them the demand of the Great Father's servant. We knew well that the country between us and Fort Berthold, about one hundred and fifty miles distant, was alive with hostile Sioux, and that if any of us should be caught and recognized by them, he would surely be put to death. It would not be easy to deceive them by professing hostility to the Government, for the record of each individual Indian is well known. The warriors were still unwilling to go, for they argued thus: 'This is a white man's errand, and will not be recorded as a brave deed upon the honor roll of our people.' I think many would have volunteered but for that belief. At that time we had not a high opinion of the white man.

"Since all the rest were silent, it came into my mind to offer my services. The warriors looked at me in astonishment, for I was a very young man and had no experience.

"Our chief, Two Bears, who was my own uncle, finally presented my name to the commanding officer. He praised my courage and begged me to be vigilant. The interpreter told him that I had never been upon the war-path and would be knocked over like a rabbit, but as no one else would go, he was obliged to accept me as his messenger. He gave me a fine horse and saddle; also a rifle and soldier's uniform. I would not take the gun nor wear the blue coat. I accepted only a revolver, and I took my bow and quiver full of arrows, and wore my usual dress. I hid the letter in my moccasin.

"I set out before daybreak the next morning. The snow was deep. I rode up the river, on the west bank, keeping a very close watch all the way, but seeing nothing. I had been provided with a pair of field glasses, and I surveyed the country on all sides from the top of every hill. Having traveled all day and part of the night, I rested my horse and I took a little sleep.

"After eating a small quantity of pemmican, I made a very early start in the morning. It was scarcely light when I headed for a near-by ridge from which to survey the country beyond. Just as I ascended the rise I found myself almost surrounded by loose ponies, evidently belonging to a winter camp of the hostile Sioux.

"I readjusted my saddle, tightened the girths, and prepared to ride swiftly around the camp. I saw some men already out after ponies. No one appeared to have seen me as yet, but I felt that as soon as it became lighter they could not help observing me. I turned to make the circuit of the camp, which was a very large one, and as soon as I reached the timbered bottom lands I began to congratulate myself that I had not been seen.

"As I entered the woods at the crossing of a dry creek, I noticed that my horse was nervous. I knew that horses are quick to discover animals or men by scent, and I became nervous, too.

"The animal put his four feet together and almost slid down the steep bank. As he came out on the opposite side he swerved suddenly and started to run. Then I saw a man watching me from behind a tree. Fortunately for me, he carried no weapon. He was out after ponies, and had only a lariat wound upon one shoulder.

"He beckoned and made signs for me to stop, but I spurred my horse and took flight at once. I could hear him yelling far behind me, no doubt to arouse the camp and set them on my trail.

"As I fled westward, I came upon another man, mounted, and driving his ponies before him. He yelled and hooted in vain; then turned and rode after me. Two others had started in pursuit, but my horse was a good one, and I easily outdistanced them at the start.

"After I had fairly circled the camp, I turned again toward the river, hoping to regain the bottom lands. The traveling was bad. Sometimes we came to deep gulches filled with snow, where my horse would sink in up to his body and seem unable to move. When I jumped off his back and struck him once or twice, he would make several desperate leaps and recover his footing. My pursuers were equally hindered, but by this time the pursuit was general, and in order to terrify me they yelled continually and fired their guns into the air. Now and then I came to a gulch which I had to follow up in search of a place to cross, and at such times they gained on me. I began to despair, for I knew that the white man's horses have not the endurance of our Indian ponies, and I expected to be chased most of the day.

"Finally I came to a ravine that seemed impossible to cross. As I followed it up, it became evident that some of them had known of this trap, and had cut in ahead of me. I felt that I must soon abandon my horse and slide down the steep sides of the gulch to save myself.

"However, I made one last effort to pass my enemies. They came within gunshot and several fired at me, although all our horses were going at full speed. They missed me, and being at last clear of them, I came to a place where I could cross, and the pursuit stopped."

When Zuyamani reached this point in his recital, the great drum was struck several times, and all the men cheered him.

"The days are short in winter," he went on after a short pause, "and just now the sun sank behind the hills. I did not linger. I continued my journey by night, and reached Fort Berthold before midnight. I had been so thoroughly frightened and was so much exhausted that I did not want to talk, and as soon as I had delivered my letters to the post commander, I went to the interpreter's quarters to sleep.

"The interpreter, however, announced my arrival, and that same night many Ree, Gros Ventre, and Mandan warriors came to call upon me. Among them was a great chief of the Rees, called Poor Dog.

"'You must be,' said he to me, 'either a very young man, or a fool! You have not told us about your close escape, but a runner came in at dusk and told us of the pursuit. He reported that you had been killed by the hostiles, for he heard many guns fired about the middle of the afternoon. These white men will never give you any credit for your wonderful ride, nor will they compensate you for the risks you have taken in their service. They will not give you so much as one eagle feather for what you have done!'

"The next day I was sent for to go to headquarters, and there I related my all-day pursuit by the hostile Sioux. The commanding officer advised me to remain at the fort fifteen days before making the return trip, thinking that by that time my enemies might cease to look for me.

"At the end of the fortnight he wrote his letters, and I told him that I was ready to start. 'I will give you,' he said, 'twenty Rees and Gros Ventres to escort you past the hostile camp.' We set out very early and rode all day, so that night overtook us just before we reached the camp.

"At nightfall we sent two scouts ahead, but before they left us they took the oath of the pipe in token of their loyalty. You all know the ancient war custom. A lighted pipe was held toward them and each one solemnly touched it, after which it was passed as usual.

"We followed more slowly, and at about midnight we came to the place where our scouts had agreed to meet us. They were to return from a reconnaissance of the camp and report on what they had seen. It was a lonely spot, and the night was very cold and still. We sat there in the snowy woods near a little creek and smoked in silence while we waited. I had plenty of time to reflect upon my position. These Gros Ventres and Rees have been our enemies for generations. I was one man to twenty! They had their orders from the commander of the fort, and that was my only safeguard.

"Soon we heard the howl of a wolf a little to the westward. Immediately one of the party answered in the same manner. I could not have told it from the howl of a real wolf. Then we heard a hooting owl down the creek. Another of our party hooted like an owl.

"Presently the wolf's voice sounded nearer, while the owl's hoot came nearer in the opposite direction. Then we heard the footsteps of ponies on the crisp, frosty air. The scout who had been imitating the wolf came in first, and the owl soon followed. The warriors made a ring and again filled the pipe, and the scouts took the oath for the second time.

"After smoking, they reported a trail going up a stream tributary to the Missouri, but whether going out or coming in it was impossible to tell in the dark. It was several days old. This was discussed for some time. The question was whether some had gone out in search of meat, or whether some additional men had come into camp.

"The Bunch of Stars was already a little west of the middle sky when we set out again. They agreed to take me a short distance beyond this creek and there leave me, as they were afraid to go any further. On the bank of the creek we took a farewell smoke. There was a faint glow in the east, showing that it was almost morning. The warriors sang a 'Strong Heart' song for me in an undertone as I went on alone.

"I tried to make a wide circuit of the camp, but I passed their ponies grazing all over the side hills at a considerable distance, and I went as quietly as possible, so as not to frighten them. When I had fairly passed the camp I came down to the road again, and I let my horse fly!

"I had been cautioned at the post that the crossings of the creeks on either side of the camp were the most dangerous places, since they would be likely to watch for me there. I had left the second crossing far behind, and I felt quite safe; but I was tired and chilled by the long ride. My horse, too, began to show signs of fatigue. In a deep ravine where there was plenty of dry wood and shelter, I cleared the ground of snow and kindled a small fire. Then I gave the horse his last ration of oats, and I ate the last of the pemmican that the Ree scouts had given me.

"Suddenly he pricked up his ears in the direction of home. He ate a mouthful and listened again. I began to grow nervous, and I listened, too. Soon I heard the footsteps of horses in the snow at a considerable distance.

"Hastily I mounted and took flight along the ravine until I had to come out upon the open plain, in full view of a party of about thirty Sioux in war-paint, coming back from the direction of Fort Rice. They immediately gave chase, yelling and flourishing their guns and tomahawks over their heads. I urged my horse to his best speed, for I felt that if they should overtake me, nothing could save me! My friend, White Elk, here, was one of that warparty.

"I saw that I had a fair lead and the best horse, and was gaining upon them, when about two miles out I met some more of the party who had lingered behind the rest. I was surrounded!

"I turned toward the north, to a deep gulch that I knew I should find there, and I led my horse along a narrow and slippery ridge to a deep hole. Here I took up my position. I guarded the pass with my bow and arrows, and they could not reach me unless they should follow the ridge in single file. I knew that they would not storm my position, for that is not the Indian way of fighting, but I supposed that they would try to tire me out. They yelled and hooted, and shot many bullets and arrows over my head to terrify me into surrender, but I remained motionless and silent.

"Night came, with a full round moon. All was light as day except the place where I stood, half frozen and not daring to move. The bottom of the gulch was as black as a well and almost as cold. The wolves howled all around me in the stillness. At last I heard the footsteps of horses retreating, and then no other sound. Still I dared not come out. I must have slept, for it was dawn when I seemed to hear faintly the yelling of warriors, and then I heard my own name.

"'Zuyamani, tokiya nunka huwo?' (Where are you, Zuyamani?) they shouted. A party of my friends had come out to meet me and had followed our trail. I was scarcely able to walk when I came out, but they filled the pipe and held it up to me, as is done in recognition of distinguished service. They escorted me into the post, singing war songs and songs of brave deeds, and there I delivered up his letters to the Chief Soldier."

Again the drum was struck and the old men cheered Zuyamani, who added:

"I think that Poor Dog was right, for the Great Father never gave me any credit, nor did he ever reward me for what I had done. Yet I have not been without honor, for my own people have not forgotten me, even though I went upon the white man's errand."

VII
THE GRAVE OF THE DOG

The full moon was just clear of the high mountain ranges. Surrounded by a ring of bluish haze, it looked almost as if it were frozen against the impalpable blueblack of the reckless midwinter sky.

The game scout moved slowly homeward, well wrapped in his long buffalo robe, which was securely belted to his strong loins; his quiver tightly tied to his shoulders so as not to impede his progress. It was enough to carry upon his feet two strong snow-shoes; for the snow was deep and its crust too thin to bear his weight.

As he emerged from the lowlands into the upper regions, he loomed up a gigantic figure against the clear, moonlit horizon. His picturesque foxskin cap with all its trimmings was incrusted with frost from the breath of his nostrils, and his lagging footfall sounded crisply. The distance he had that day covered was enough for any human endurance; yet he was neither faint nor hungry; but his feet were frozen into the psay, the snow-shoes, so that he could not run faster than an easy slip and slide.

At last he reached the much-coveted point—the crown of the last ascent; and when he smelled fire and the savory odor of the jerked buffalo meat, it well-nigh caused him to waver! But he must not fail to follow the custom of untold ages, and give the game scout's wolf call before entering camp.

Accordingly he paused upon the highest point of the ridge and uttered a cry to which the hungry cry of a real wolf would have seemed but a coyote's yelp in comparison! Then it was that the rest of the buffalo hunters knew that their game scout was returning with welcome news; for the unsuccessful scout enters the camp silently.

A second time he gave the call to assure his hearers that their ears did not deceive them. The gray wolves received the news with perfect understanding. It meant food! "Woo-o-o-o! woo-o-o-o!" came from all directions, especially from the opposite ridge. Thus the ghostly, cold, weird night was enlivened with the music from many wild throats.

Down the gradual slope the scout hastened; his footfall was the only sound that broke the stillness after the answers to his call had ceased. As he crossed a little ridge an immense wolf suddenly confronted him, and instead of retreating, calmly sat up and gazed steadfastly into his face.

"Welcome, welcome, friend!" the hunter spoke as he passed.

In the meantime, the hunters at the temporary camp were aroused to a high pitch of excitement. Some turned their buffalo robes and put them on in such a way as to convert themselves into make-believe bison, and began to tread the snow, while others were singing the buffalo song, that their spirits might be charmed and allured within the circle of the camp-fires. The scout, too, was singing his buffalo bull song in a guttural, lowing chant as he neared the hunting camp. Within arrow-shot he paused again, while the usual ceremonies were enacted for his reception. This done, he was seated with the leaders in a chosen place.

"It was a long run," he said, "but there were no difficulties. I found the first herd directly north of here. The second herd, a great one, is northeast, near Shell Lake. The snow is deep. The buffalo can only follow their leader in their retreat."

"Hi, hi, hi!" the hunters exclaimed solemnly in token of gratitude, raising their hands heavenward and then pointing them toward the ground.

"Ho, kola! one more round of the buffalo-pipe, then we shall retire, to rise before daybreak for the hunt," advised one of the leaders. Silently they partook in turn of the long-stemmed pipe, and one by one, with a dignified "Ho!" departed to their teepees.

The scout betook himself to his little old buffalo teepee, which he used for winter hunting expeditions. His faithful Shunka, who had been all this time its only occupant, met him at the entrance as dogs alone know how to welcome a lifelong friend. As his master entered he stretched himself in his old-time way, from the tip of his tail to that of his tongue, and finished by curling both ends upward.

"Ho, mita shunka, eat this; for you must be hungry!" So saying, the scout laid before his canine friend the last piece of his dried buffalo meat. It was the sweetest meal ever eaten by a dog, judging by his long smacking of his lips after he had swallowed it!

The hunting party was soon lost in heavy slumber. Not a sound could be heard save the gnawing of the ponies upon the cottonwood bark, which was provided for them instead of hay in the winter time.

All about Shell Lake the bison were gathered in great herds. The unmistakable signs of the sky had warned them of approaching bad weather. The moon's robe was girdled with the rainbow wampum of heaven. The very music of the snow under their feet had given them warning. On the north side of Shell Lake there were several deep gulches, which were the homes of every wanderer of the plains at such a time at this. When there was a change toward severe weather, all the four-footed people headed for this lake. Here was a heavy growth of reeds, rushes, and coarse grass, making good shelters, and also springs, which afforded water after the lake was frozen solid. Hence great numbers of the bison had gathered here.

When Wapashaw, the game scout, had rolled himself in his warm buffalo robe and was sound asleep, his faithful companion hunter, the great Esquimaux wolf dog, silently rose and again stretched himself, then stood quiet for a moment as if meditating. It was clear that he knew well what he had planned to do, but was considering how he should do it without arousing any suspicion of his movements. This is a dog's art, and the night tricks and marauding must always be the joy and secret of his life!

Softly he emerged from the lodge and gave a sweeping glance around to assure him that there were none to spy upon him. Suspiciously he sniffed the air, as if to ascertain whether there could be any danger to his sleeping master while he should be away.

His purpose was still a secret. It may be that it was not entirely a selfish one, or merely the satisfying of his inherited traits. Having fully convinced himself of the safety of the unguarded camp, he went forth into the biting cold. The moon was now well up on the prairies of the sky. There were no cloud hills in the blue field above to conceal her from view. Her brilliant light set on fire every snow gem upon the plains and hillsides about the hunters' camp.

Up the long ascent he trotted in a northerly direction, yet not following his master's trail. He was large and formidable in strength, combining the features of his wild brothers of the plains with those of the dogs who keep company with the red men. His jet-black hair and sharp ears and nose appeared to immense advantage against the spotless and jeweled snow, until presently his own warm breath had coated him with heavy frost.

After a time Shunka struck into his master's trail and followed it all the way, only taking a short cut here and there when by dog instinct he knew that a man must go around such a point to get to his destination. He met many travelers during the night, but none had dared to approach him, though some few followed at a distance, as if to discover his purpose.

At last he reached Shell Lake, and there beheld a great gathering of the herds! They stood in groups, like enormous rocks, no longer black, but white with frost. Every one of them emitted a white steam, quickly frozen into a fine snow in the air.

Shunka sat upon his haunches and gazed.

"Wough, this is it!" he said to himself. He had kept still when the game scout gave the wolf call, though the camp was in an uproar, and from the adjacent hills the wild hunters were equally joyous, because they understood the meaning of the unwonted noise. Yet his curiosity was not fully satisfied, and he had set out to discover the truth, and it may be to protect or serve his master in case of danger.

At daybreak the great dog meekly entered his master's rude teepee, and found him already preparing for the prospective hunt. He was filling his inside moccasins full of buffalo hair to serve as stockings, over which he put on his large buffalo moccasins with the hair inside, and adjusted his warm leggings. He then adjusted his snowshoes and filled his quiver full of good arrows. The dog quietly lay down in a warm place, making himself as small as possible, as if to escape observation, and calmly watched his master.

"Ho, ho, ho, kola! Enakanee, enakanee!" shouted the game herald. "It is always best to get the game early; then their spirits can take flight with the coming of a new day!"

All had now donned their snow-shoes. There was no food left; therefore no delay to prepare breakfast.

"It is very propitious for our hunt," one exclaimed; "everything is in our favor. There is a good crust on the snow, and the promise of a good clear day!"

Soon all the hunters were running in single file upon the trail of the scout, each Indian closely followed by his trusty hunting dog. In less than two hours they stood just back of the low ridge which rounded the south side of Shell Lake. The narrow strip of land between its twin divisions was literally filled with the bison. In the gulches beyond, between the dark lines of timber, there were also scattered groups; but the hunters at once saw their advantage over the herd upon the peninsula.

"Hechetu, kola! This is well, friends!" exclaimed the first to speak. "These can be forced to cross the slippery ice and the mire around the springs. This will help us to get more meat. Our people are hungry, and we must kill many in order to feed them!"

"Ho, ho, ho!" agreed all the hunters.

"And it is here that we can use our companion hunters best, for the shunkas will intimidate and bewilder the buffalo women," said an old man.

"Ugh, he is always right! Our dogs must help us here. The meat will be theirs as well as ours," another added.

"Tosh, kola! The game scout's dog is the greatest shunka of them all! He has a mind near like that of a man. Let him lead the attack of his fellows, while we crawl up on the opposite side and surround the buffalo upon the slippery ice and in the deceitful mire," spoke up a third. So it was agreed that the game scout and his Shunka should lead the attack of the dogs.

"Woo, woo, woo!" was the hoarse signal from the throat of the game scout; but his voice was drowned by the howling and barking of the savage dogs as they made their charge. In a moment all was confusion among the buffalo. Some started this way, others that, and the great mass swayed to and fro uncertainly. A few were ready to fight, but the snow was too deep for a countercharge upon the dogs, save on the ice just in front of them, where the wind had always full sweep. There all was slippery and shining! In their excitement and confusion the bison rushed upon this uncertain plain.

Their weight and the momentum of their rush carried them hopelessly far out, where they were again confused as to which way to go, and many were stuck in the mire which was concealed by the snow, except here and there an opening above a spring from which there issued a steaming vapor. The game scout and his valiant dog led on the force of canines with deafening war-cries, and one could see black heads here and there popping from behind the embankments. As the herd finally swept toward the opposite shore, many dead were left behind. Pierced by the arrows of the hunters, they lay like black mounds upon the glassy plain.

It was a great hunt! "Once more the camp will be fed," they thought, "and this good fortune will help us to reach the spring alive!"

A chant of rejoicing rang out from the opposite shore, while the game scout unsheathed his big knife and began the work which is ever the sequel of the hunt—to dress the game; although the survivors of the slaughter had scarcely disappeared behind the hills. The dogs had all run back to their respective masters, and this left the scout and his companion Shunka alone. Some were appointed to start a camp in a neighboring gulch among the trees, so that the hunters might bring their meat there and eat before setting out for the great camp on the Big River.

All were busily skinning and cutting up the meat into pieces convenient for carrying, when suddenly a hunter called the attention of those near him to an ominous change in the atmosphere.

"There are signs of a blizzard! We must hurry into the near woods before it reaches us!" he shouted.

Some heard him; others did not. Those who saw or heard passed on the signal and hurried toward the wood, where others had already arranged rude shelters and gathered piles of dry wood for fuel.

Around the several camp-fires the hunters sat or stood, while slices of savory meat were broiled and eaten with a relish by the half-starved men.

"Ho, kola! Eat this, friend!" said they to one another as one finished broiling a steak of the bison and offered it to his neighbor.

But the storm had now fairly enveloped them in whirling whiteness. "Woo, woo!" they called to those who had not yet reached camp. One after another answered and emerged from the blinding pall of snow. At last none were missing save the game scout and his Shunka!

The hunters passed the time in eating and telling stories until a late hour, occasionally giving a united shout to guide the lost one should he chance to pass near their camp.

"Fear not for our scout, friends!" finally exclaimed a leader among them. "He is a brave and experienced man. He will find a safe resting-place, and join us when the wind ceases to rage." So they all wrapped themselves in their robes and lay down to sleep.

All that night and the following day it was impossible to give succor, and the hunters felt much concern for the absent. Late in the second night the great storm subsided.

"Ho, ho! Iyotanka! Rise up!" So the first hunter to awaken aroused all the others.

As after every other storm, it was wonderfully still; so still that one could hear distinctly the pounding feet of the jack-rabbits coming down over the slopes to the willows for food. All dry vegetation was buried beneath the deep snow, and everywhere they saw this white-robed creature of the prairie coming down to the woods.

Now the air was full of the wolf and coyote game call, and they were seen in great numbers upon the ice.

"See, see! the hungry wolves are dragging the carcasses away! Harken to the war cries of the scout's Shunka! Hurry, hurry!" they urged one another in chorus.

Away they ran and out upon the lake; now upon the wind-swept ice, now upon the crusted snow; running when they could, sliding when they must. There was certainly a great concourse of the wolves, whirling in frantic circles, but continually moving toward the farther end of the lake. They could hear distinctly the hoarse bark of the scout's Shunka, and occasionally the muffled war-whoop of a man, as if it came from under the ice!

As they approached nearer the scene they could hear more distinctly the voice of their friend, but still as it were from underground. When they reached the spot to which the wolves had dragged two of the carcasses of the buffalo, Shunka was seen to stand by one of them, but at that moment he staggered and fell. The hunters took out their knives and ripped up the frozen hide covering the abdominal cavity. It revealed a warm nest of hay and buffalo hair in which the scout lay, wrapped in his own robe!

He had placed his dog in one of the carcasses and himself in another for protection from the storm; but the dog was wiser than the man, for he kept his entrance open. The man lapped the hide over and it froze solidly, shutting him securely in. When the hungry wolves came Shunka promptly extricated himself and held them off as long as he could; meanwhile, sliding and pulling, the wolves continued to drag over the slippery ice the body of the buffalo in which his master had taken refuge. The poor, faithful dog, with no care for his own safety, stood by his imprisoned master until the hunters came up. But it was too late, for he had received more than one mortal wound.

As soon as the scout got out, with a face more anxious for another than for himself, he exclaimed:

"Where is Shunka, the bravest of his tribe?"

"Ho, kola, it is so, indeed; and here he lies," replied one sadly.

His master knelt by his side, gently stroking the face of the dog.

"Ah, my friend; you go where all spirits live! The Great Mystery has a home for every living creature. May he permit our meeting there!"

At daybreak the scout carried him up to one of the pretty round hills overlooking the lake, and built up around him walls of loose stone. Red paints were scattered over the snow, in accordance with Indian custom, and the farewell song was sung.

Since that day the place has been known to the Sioux as Shunkahanakapi—the Grave of the Dog.

www.ingramcontent.com/pod-product-compliance
Lightning Source LLC
LaVergne TN
LVHW091622170726
843492LV00007B/2553